English 365

Student's Book 1

PUBLISHED BY THE PRESS SYNDICATE OF THE UNIVERSITY OF CAMBRIDGE
The Pitt Building, Trumpington Street, Cambridge, United Kingdom

CAMBRIDGE UNIVERSITY PRESS
The Edinburgh Building, Cambridge CB2 2RU, UK
40 West 20th Street, New York, NY 10011–4211, USA
477 Williamstown Road, Port Melbourne, VIC 3207, Australia
Ruiz de Alarcón 13, 28014 Madrid, Spain
Dock House, The Waterfront, Cape Town 8001, South Africa

http://www.cambridge.org
http://www.cambridge.org/elt/english365

First published 2004

Printed in the United Kingdom at the University Press, Cambridge

Typeface Swift *System* QuarkXpress® [HMCL]

A catalogue record for this book is available from the British Library

ISBN 0 521 75362 7 Student's Book 1
ISBN 0 521 75363 5 Teacher's Book 1
ISBN 0 521 75364 3 Personal Study Book 1 with Audio CD
ISBN 0 521 75365 1 Student's Book 1 Audio Cassette Set
ISBN 0 521 75366 X Student's Book 1 Audio CD Set

CAMBRIDGE Professional English

for work and life

English 365

Student's Book 1

Bob Dignen Steve Flinders Simon Sweeney

CAMBRIDGE
UNIVERSITY PRESS

Contents

To the student

Who is *English365* for?

Welcome to *English365*. *English365* is for people who need English for their jobs and for their free time. If you use English at work and also when you travel and meet people, *English365* is for you. *English365* is for and about real working people and every unit gives you English which you can use straightaway at work or in your free time.

What is *English365*?

There are two main parts to this course:

The **Student's Book**, which you are reading now. There are also classroom cassettes or audio CDs for the listening exercises in this book.

The **Personal Study Book with Audio CD** is to help you remember the English which you learn in the classroom. The more you work outside the classroom, the better your English.

- The Personal Study Book has important information about the language, and exercises for you to practise.
- The Audio CDs give you extra listening practice. You can also practise the Student's Book pronunciation exercises and the social English dialogues on your own.

What's in the Student's Book?

With the Student's Book, you can work on:

- the **grammar** which you need to make English work for you
- the **vocabulary** you need for your job and for your free time
- the **phrases** you need for your free time – at the airport, in a hotel, etc.
- the **phrases** you need for your work – telephoning, emailing, etc.
- **pronunciation** rules to help you speak better and understand better too.

There are 30 units in the book (plus two revision units, one after Unit 15 and one after Unit 30), and there are three types of unit:
Type 1 units (Units 1, 4, 7, etc. – the purple units)
Type 2 units (Units 2, 5, 8, etc. – the blue units)
Type 3 units (Units 3, 6, 9, etc. – the green units)

In **type 1** units you work mainly on:

- Listening
- Grammar
- Pronunciation.

In **type 2** units, you work mainly on:

- Reading
- Vocabulary for **work**
- Communication skills for **work** – for telephoning, writing emails, meeting visitors, etc.

In **type 3** units, you work mainly on:

- Phrases for **travel and socialising**
- Listening
- Vocabulary for your **free time**.

You practise **speaking** in every unit!

At the back of the book, there are also:

- File cards for pairwork exercises (page 104)
- Grammar notes (page 110)
- The tapescripts for the classroom cassettes/audio CDs (page 121)
- Answers to all the exercises (page 135)

We hope you enjoy learning with *English365*. We had fun writing it. Good luck with your English.

Bob Dignen

Steve Flinders

Simon Sweeney

On the agenda

Speaking
Meeting people

Grammar
The present simple 1

Pronunciation
Reply questions

Meet Susie Smith. She works for Skateline. Her company sells inline skates.

1 Nice to meet you

Warm up

Read these two introductions:

" A: Hi, I'm Susie.

B: Hi, I'm Masahiko Kamiya, from Japan. "

" C: Hello. My name's Françoise, Françoise Duroc from FranceCom. Nice to meet you.

D: Good morning. Herr Wollmann from KV Bonn. "

1 Which introduction is more formal?
2 What do you say when you welcome visitors at work?
3 Introduce yourself to the other people in your group.

Listen to this

Say who you are

1 Susie is on the Skateline stand at Expo – the International Sportex Show. She makes notes about all the people she meets. Listen to her talking at the stand. Tick (✓) the correct details about her visitor. ▶▶|1.1

Name:	Paula Visconti	
	Olga Novotna	
	Lena Molnar	
Visitor from:	Hungary	
	Russia	
	Italy	
Company activity:	Sportswear	
	Skiing equipment	
	Bicycles	
Action:	Send email	
	Arrange meeting	
	No action	

Inline skates

2 Listen again. Are these sentences about Susie's visitor true or false? ▶▶|1.1

		T	F
1	It is her first visit to Expo	☐	☐
2	Her home is 100 kilometres from Moscow.	☐	☐
3	Technosport is in Moscow.	☐	☐
4	She doesn't want a brochure.	☐	☐

The present simple 1

We can use the present simple to ask and answer questions when we meet people.
Complete the questions and answers below.

Question	Positive	Negative
Where (1) .... you live?	I live in Rome.	I don't live in Barcelona.

Look at the verb *to be*.

Where (2) .... you from?	I'm from Spain.	I'm not from Italy.
What (3) .... your job?	I'm a personal assistant.	I (4) .... not responsible for sales.
Are you from Rome?	Yes, I (5)	No, I'm not.

Now look at two different ways you can use the verb *to have*.

Do you (6) .... a brochure?	Yes, I (7)	No, I don't.
(8) .... you got a brochure?	Yes, I have.	No, I haven't.

Grammar reference page 111 ▶

Do it yourself

1 Correct the mistakes in these sentences.

  1 Do ~~he~~ *you* ~~working~~ for IBM? *Do you work for IBM?*

  2 Has you children?

  3 I doesn't work in Paris.

  4 We working near Milan.

2 Match the beginnings and endings.

  1 I work for ...   ... the north of England originally.
  2 I come from ...   ... a personal assistant.
  3 I live in ...   ... about six times a year on business.
  4 I'm ...   ... a British company.
  5 I go to the US ...   ... Croydon, about 20 kilometres from London.

3 Match each question below (a–e) with one of the sentences above (1–5).

  a Do you travel much in your job?
  b What do you do?
  c Who do you work for?
  d Where do you live?
  e Where are you from?

Now ask your partner the same questions.

And where do you come from?

4 Complete the conversation between Susie and Maria, another visitor at the International Sportex show.

SUSIE: So, where (1) .... you from, Maria?

MARIA: (2) .... from Italy.

SUSIE: Really? Are you (3) .... Rome?

MARIA: No, I'm not. I'm from Milan. (4) .... you know Milan?

SUSIE: Yes, I went there on holiday last year. It's a lovely place.

MARIA: Yes, it's beautiful. Do you (5) .... to Italy often?

SUSIE: No, I (6) .... travel much, maybe two or three times a year for business.

MARIA: Which company do you (7) .... for?

SUSIE: I work for Skateline.

MARIA: Skateline? Yes, I know the name. What (8) .... you do exactly?

SUSIE: We (9) .... inline skates. And you? What do you do?

MARIA: We (10) .... bicycles.

Now listen and check. ▶▶1.2

from
work
sell
Do
don't
I'm
make
do
come
are

Reply questions

When someone asks you a question in conversation, you can ask the same question back to show interest in the other person. When you do this, it's important to stress the *you* in your question.

1 Listen to Susie pronounce the *you* in this conversation. Then practise the conversation with a partner. ▶▶|1.3

MARIA: What do you do exactly?

SUSIE: We make inline skates. And *you*? What do *you* do?

MARIA: We sell bicycles.

2 Make similar conversations with these questions. Practise with your partner.

1 Where do you live?
2 What do you do?
3 Do you travel much in your job?
4 Do you play tennis?
5 Which company do you work for?

It's time to talk

Get to know the other people in the room, asking and answering questions about their job, organisation, family and home.

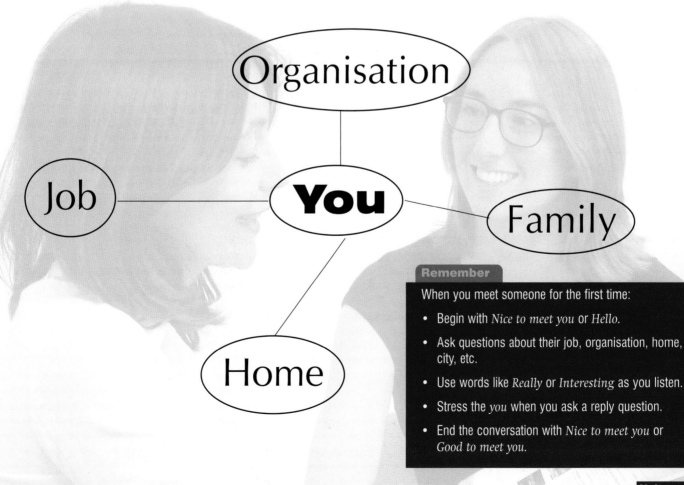

Organisation

Job — **You** — Family

Home

Remember

When you meet someone for the first time:

- Begin with *Nice to meet you* or *Hello.*

- Ask questions about their job, organisation, home, city, etc.

- Use words like *Really* or *Interesting* as you listen.

- Stress the *you* when you ask a reply question.

- End the conversation with *Nice to meet you* or *Good to meet you.*

On the agenda

Speaking
Your job

Vocabulary
Job responsibilities

Communicating at work
Telephoning 1: Getting information

Meet Bonnie Bernström. She works for Språngbrädan, a consulting company with a difference.

2 Helping people to learn

Warm up

Read what some people say about their work. Do you think the same?

I like working for a small company. It's more friendly.

I love writing and receiving emails. I like communicating!

I want to travel in my job. Work with no travel is boring.

Read on

A new future

1 We interviewed Bonnie about her job. Match our questions to Bonnie's answers.

1 Which organisation do you work for?

2 What do you do?

3 Tell me about a typical day at work.

4 What do you like about your job? What don't you like?

A I think the best thing about my job is meeting people because it's nice to make new friends. I also like the email communication with the women I work with in Eastern Europe. We write every week just to say hello. That's really nice. One thing I don't like is writing reports. I work a lot on projects so I write a lot of project reports, which is very boring!

B Every day is different. There is no typical day! But I travel a lot to places like Moldova or Ukraine where I usually meet people and talk about political problems for women in these countries – that kind of thing. But this week is good – I have no business trips!

C Well, I'm part of a consulting company in Sweden called Språngbrädan, that's 'springboard' in English. We are active in eight countries and we work with money we get from the European Union for our projects. We are small at the moment, with four employees, who are all women.

D Well, I'm a consultant and I give training to women and men in the former Soviet Union countries about politics. I'm responsible for helping women to begin in politics, both locally and nationally. We discuss problems a lot and think about how to make a new future. My target is to help 100% more women into politics in these countries.

2 Read the text again and answer these questions about Bonnie.

1 What is Bonnie's main responsibility?

2 Where does Bonnie travel for her job?

3 How many people work for Språngbrädan?

4 What does Bonnie like most about her job?

What do you think? Would you like to do Bonnie's job? What do you like about your job? What don't you like?

The words you need ... to talk about your job

1 Choose the correct prepositions in these sentences about Bonnie.

1	I'm part	of / for	a consulting company.
2	I work	on / for	Språngbrädan.
3	I work	in / at	training.
4	I'm responsible	of / for	developing democracy.
5	I work closely	with / for	three female colleagues.
6	I'm in charge	for / of	Eastern Europe.
7	An important part	of / at	my job is email contact.
8	I work	at / in	the former Soviet Union.

Now listen and check your answers. Then make similar sentences about yourself. ▶▶ 2.1

2 It is important to use nouns and verbs correctly.

Example: Verb – *train*   I *train* women.
Noun – *training*   I do a lot of *training*.

Choose the correct noun or verb in these sentences.

1 I *meet / meeting* a lot of people in my job.

2 I work for a small *organise / organisation*.

3 I *communicate / communication* a lot by email.

4 I *manage / management* a small team of three women.

5 I have a lot of political *discuss / discussions* in my job.

3 Make questions with the verbs and nouns above.
Ask your partner your questions.

Question: Do you meet a lot of people in your job?

Answer: Yes, I do. / No, I don't.

It's time to talk

Ask your partner about his/her job and organisation. Look back at some of the questions in this unit and in Unit 1 to help you. Note down your partner's answers in the table.

Work		Company/organisation	
Job title		Name	
Main responsibility		Activity	
One thing I like in my job		Number of employees	
Other information		Other information	

Communicating at work

Telephoning 1: Getting information

1 Listen to two telephone calls Peter Blake gets about a training course. Write the number of the call next to the information below. Write ✗ if the information isn't in either call. ▶▶|2.2

Caller		Reason		Result	
Jake Roberts	☐	Cancel training	☐	Call back in ten minutes	☐
Jane Dawson	☐	Discuss a problem	☐	No action – talk next week	☐
Julie Simpson	☐	Give help	☐	Send email with information	☐

2 Listen again. Which of these sentences do you hear? ▶▶|2.2

A Answering a phone call

Good morning. How can I help you? ☐

Who's calling, please? ☐

Connecting you now. ☐

I'll put you through. ☐

B Introducing yourself

My name's … (+name) ☐

It's … (+ name) ☐

C Giving a reason for the call

Could I speak to … (+ name)? ☐

I'm just calling to … (+ reason for call) ☐

Could you … (+ reason for call) ☐

D Finish the call

Thanks for calling. ☐

Talk to you next week. Bye. ☐

Which do you prefer – call 1 or call 2? Why?

3 Are you good on the phone? Look at this plan for making good phone calls.

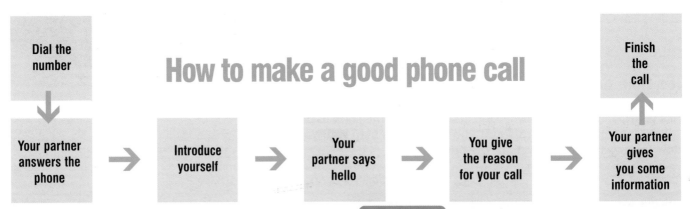

How to make a good phone call

Dial the number → Your partner answers the phone → Introduce yourself → Your partner says hello → You give the reason for your call → Your partner gives you some information → Finish the call

Practise making two phone calls with your partner. Use the plan to help you make your calls. Student A should look at page 104, and Student B at page 106.

Remember

When you talk on the phone in English:
- Speak your name slowly and clearly: My name is …
- Say clearly the reason for your call: I'm calling to …
- End positively: Thanks.

On the agenda

Speaking
Weekends

Social phrases
At the office

Vocabulary
Your free time

Warm up

When does your weekend begin?
When does it finish?

3 Have a good weekend

It's almost the weekend

1 Complete the dialogues with phrases (a–h) below.

Arriving at the office on Friday

A: Hi, John.
B: Morning. How are you?
A: (1) .... ?
B: Not bad. A bit tired.
A: (2) .... It's almost the weekend.

Going for lunch

A: Ready for some lunch?
B: (3) ....
A: Where do you want to eat?
B: (4) .... ?
A: Yes, it's Friday. The new Italian place?
B: Great. Let's go.

A weekend away

A: Do you have any plans for the weekend?
B: I'm going to visit my brother.
A: (5) .... ?
B: In Stratford-upon-Avon.
A: Stratford? It's a lovely place.
   (6) .... !
B: Thanks. I will!

Going home

A: I'm going. See you next week.
B: (7) ....
A: Have a good weekend.
B: Thanks. (8) .... Bye.

a Shall we eat out

b Yes, good idea

c Never mind

d You too

e Fine, thanks. And you

f OK, see you

g Have a good time

h Where does he live

Have a go

Cover the dialogues above and make your own, starting with the words below.

Arriving at the office

Hi ...

Going for lunch

Ready for ...

A weekend away

Do you have any plans for ... ?

Going home

I'm going. See you ...

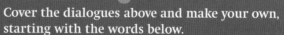

2 Now listen and check. ▶▶3.1

3 Practise reading the dialogues with a partner.

Listen to this

Enjoying your weekend

Jochen
Hinawi
Martina
Sally

Meet Sally, Hinawi, Martina and Jochen. Find out how they enjoy their weekends.

1 Look at the activities below. Do you do any of these things?

visiting friends

sightseeing

scuba diving

walking

flying

sailing

going to the cinema

swimming

clubbing

astronomy

2 Now listen to Sally, Hinawi, Martina and Jochen talking about the activities they do. Match the people to the activities. You can match more than one activity to a person. ▶▶|3.2

What do you think? Listen again and decide which person has the most interesting weekend. Why? ▶▶|3.2

The words you need ... to talk about your free time

1 Look at the different activities in the box. Write them in the gaps.

Sports	football, swimming, ...*skiing*......
Card and board games	chess, poker, ...
Reading	novels, poetry, ...
Music – listening	jazz, pop, ...
Music – playing	the piano, the saxophone, ...
Culture	opera, theatre, ...
Couch potato	playing computer games, watching videos, ...
Food	Chinese, Italian, ...
Socialising	inviting friends to dinner, going to restaurants, ...
Housework	cleaning, hoovering, ...

A couch potato

draughts

surfing the net

French

ballet

ironing

non-fiction

~~skiing~~

classical music

the guitar

going on holiday with friends

Can you add one or two activities to each category?
Ask your partner to tell you one activity he/she loves and one activity he/she hates.

2 Look at these adjectives and match the opposites.

easy	horrible
expensive	terrible
dangerous	safe
interesting	cheap
fast	unhealthy
relaxing	slow
nice	bad
healthy	boring
fantastic	stressful
good	difficult

Test your partner Say one of the adjectives above. Your partner must say the opposite.

3 Now use the adjectives to make sentences about weekend activities.

Example:

"Walking is very healthy."

"Smoking is very unhealthy."

It's time to talk

Interview three partners about two of their favourite free-time activities and complete the table. Ask them *when* they do these activities and *why* they like them. Use the questions and answers below to help you.

		What	When	Why
Person A	1			
	2			
Person B	1			
	2			
Person C	1			
	2			

Questions	Answers	
What do you like doing in your free time?	I love ... ☺	I hate ... ☹
Do you like ... ?	I really like ...	I don't like ...
What are you interested in ... ?	I'm interested in ...	I'm not very interested in ...
When do you ... ?	At the weekend. / On Mondays.	
Why?	Because ...	

Remember

Remember to use *-ing* for things you love doing and hate doing:
• I love walk**ing**.
• I like / enjoy be**ing** with my family.
• I hate runn**ing**.
And ...
• I go swimm**ing** at the weekend.

On the agenda

Speaking
Work routines

Grammar
The present simple 2

Pronunciation
The present simple
third person

Meet Anneli and Chiara. Anneli works for Telia Mobile in Sweden. Chiara works for Air Liquide in Italy.

4 North and south

Listen to this

A working day in the north ... and in the south of Europe

1 We interviewed Anneli and Chiara about their working days. Look at the information about them. Then listen to them speaking and change any details which are not correct. ▶▶ **4.1**

2 Listen again. Are these sentences true or false?

1 Anneli brings food to work for lunch.   **T** ☐ **F** ☐

2 Anneli's work is sometimes stressful.   **T** ☐ **F** ☐

3 Chiara prefers working in the morning.   **T** ☐ **F** ☐

4 Chiara sometimes works at the weekend.   **T** ☐ **F** ☐

Warm up

Are you a morning person? Or are you an afternoon person?

Anneli	**Chiara**
• starts work at 8	• starts work at 9
• has lunch at 1	• has lunch at 12.30
• usually finishes work at 6	• has dinner at 8.30

What do you think? Which European working day do you prefer – the northern or the southern?

Anneli says: 'Work can be very stressful sometimes.' What is stressful in your job?

Check your grammar

The present simple 2

1 Complete the questions and answers below.

Question	Positive	Negative
When (1) .... she work?	She sometimes works on Saturday.	She (2) .... like to work at the weekend.
Does she work at the weekend?	Yes, she (3)	No, she doesn't.

Look at the verb *to be*

Is she from Milan?	Yes, she (4)	No, she isn't.

Talking about everyday routines

We can use the present simple with time adverbs (*always*, *sometimes*, etc.) and time expressions (*every year*, *twice a week*, etc.) to talk about things we do every day at work or at home.

2 Anneli says: 'I *usually* eat at eleven for one hour.' Put these time adverbs in the correct position below.

sometimes   usually   often   rarely

....

always   normally   not very often   never
100%   0%

3 Chiara says she has 'lunch around one o'clock *every day*.' Complete the time expressions below.

1 I have lunch in the canteen once or twice .... week.
2 I check my emails .... morning.
3 I travel to Brussels three .... a month.

Grammar reference pages 111–113 ▶▶▶

Do it yourself

1 Correct the mistakes in these sentences.

1 I start normally work at 7.30.

2 She travel on business once a year.

3 How often does she calls you?

4 Does you often speak English at work?

2 Complete the text below with the words in the box.

never	always	every	a	times	usually

Javier works in Barcelona.

Stopping stress

Javier's life is (1) .... very busy. He is president of his own company, Tecna, which makes equipment for farms. He doesn't begin too early because he works late (2) .... evening. He (3) .... finishes at 9 o'clock but sometimes later. Javier goes to Cuba three (4) .... a year to visit important customers. He also travels to Australia, China, Mexico and the USA, maybe 15 weeks (5) .... year. So how does he stop stress? He walks to work most days and walks home for lunch. And he (6) .... works at the weekend. This is for spending time with his family on the beach!

3 Complete these questions about Javier.

1 When / start work? When does he start work?

2 What time / do finish?

3 How often / go to Cuba?

4 Where / go at lunchtime?

5 What / do at the weekend?

Test your partner Ask your partner to close his/her book. Then ask him/her five questions about Javier. Can your partner remember the answers?

4 Match the questions (1–5) and answers (a–e).

1 Do you ever walk to work?
2 When do you normally start work?
3 How often do you go out for lunch?
4 When do you normally finish work?
5 What do you usually do in the evening?

a Not a lot. Sometimes I just listen to music.
b Before 8.30.
c No, I don't. I always drive.
d It depends but I'm normally at the office until 7.
e Never. I always have a sandwich at my desk.

Now ask your partner the same questions.

The present simple third person

Listen to the three ways in which we pronounce the third person –s in the present simple. Then say them aloud to your partner. ▶▶ 4.2

Type 1	Type 2	Type 3
/s/	/z/	/ɪz/
gets	goes	watches

Now listen to these verbs. Number them as type 1, 2 or 3. ▶▶ 4.3

leaves ▢	sells ▢	organises ▢	listens ▢
writes ▢	works ▢	meets ▢	manages ▢
relaxes ▢	buys ▢	visits ▢	does ▢

Now practise by saying all the words aloud.

It's time to talk

The Stress Check   In Britain, businesses lose €2.4 billion per year when people stay away from work because of stress. Do you have a lot of stress? Ask and answer the questions below with a partner.

Per day, how often do you:	Always	Often	Sometimes	Rarely	Never
take regular breaks?	5	4	3	2	1
work more than ten hours?	1	2	3	4	5
finish all the jobs you plan to do?	5	4	3	2	1
feel you have too much to do?	1	2	3	4	5
drink more than four cups of coffee?	1	2	3	4	5
do more than 15 minutes of physical exercise?	5	4	3	2	1
close your eyes and relax for five minutes?	5	4	3	2	1
have more than two alcoholic drinks?	1	2	3	4	5
sleep more than seven hours?	5	4	3	2	1
laugh more than ten times?	5	4	3	2	1
TOTAL	▢	▢	▢	▢	▢

Add the numbers.   **TOTAL** ▭

Now read your score on page109.

Some organisations pay for their staff to do T'ai Chi to help them with stress.

What is a good way to control stress?

> **Remember**
> When asking about routines, you can ask questions beginning:
> • How often do you … ?
> • Do you usually … ?
> And you can answer with:
> • I always/often/sometimes/never …

On the agenda

Speaking
Introducing your
organisation

Communicating at work
Telephoning 2: Taking
messages

Vocabulary
People and organisations

**Meet Margita Westring,
who works in a hospital
in Sweden.**

5 Health care – public or private?

Warm up

What do you think about hospitals in your country?
Are you happy with their quality and service?

Read on

Working at Växjö Hospital

1 We interviewed Margita Westring about her job. Match the headings
with her answers.

1 My organisation

2 Who pays the bill?

3 The customer comes first

4 Why I like the job

A It's a very modern hospital. We say it's a 'county' hospital, so it's for the whole area not just the city. We have about 2,100 employees. Most of them are nurses – there are 900 nurses and about 200 doctors and then other employees too. We also use outside consultants. I think that at the moment we have around 350 hospital beds.

B Our first objective in the hospital is to focus on our customer, the patient. It's very important to talk to patients a lot so they understand what a doctor is doing. We also always make sure patients don't stay in hospital too long. We think people prefer to be out of hospital quickly and at home.

C In Sweden, people pay 250 Swedish krona for every visit to a doctor. This is the standard cost for a national health service visit. Of course, you can go to our competitor, a private medical centre, but you pay 500 to 1,000 Swedish krona. It's a lot of money but some people are happy to pay.

D I work as a human resources officer. I like working in the public sector because I want to look after people and not only think about profit and I like the idea that everyone has the right to health care. So I plan to stay at Växjö Hospital. I always want to work in the public sector and never go into the private sector.

2 Read the text again and answer these questions.

1 How many people work at Växjö Hospital?
2 What is the most important objective for employees in Växjö Hospital?
3 How much does a national health service visit usually cost?
4 Why does Margita want to work in a public sector hospital?

What do you think? Margita says: 'I always want to work in the public sector and not go into the private sector.' Do you think it is better to work in the public or private sector?

The words you need ... to talk about people and organisations

1 Choose the correct words in these sentences about a clothing company in Paris.

1 We have over 3,000 employers / employees.

2 Our main competitor / competitive is AMCAP of the USA.

3 Most of our customs / customers are in the Paris area.

4 JCG is a very important supply / supplier for us. We buy textiles from them.

5 We sometimes use marketing consultants / consults to give us ideas.

Now make sentences about your organisation using the words you have chosen.

2 Complete the following sentences with the correct preposition from the box.

1 I work .... a human resources officer. I work with people a lot.

2 I am a customer service manager. It's my job to look .... our customers.

3 I am the chief buyer. I look .... new and cheaper suppliers all the time.

4 I am a personnel manager. I talk .... employees about personal development.

5 I am a public relations officer. I look .... the newspapers every day.

6 I am PA to the boss. I deal .... everything!

Now use some of the verbs and prepositions to make sentences about your job.

There are a lot of employees.

as	at
	to
after	for
	with

It's time to talk

1 Prepare a short introduction to your organisation.
Use the words in this unit and in Unit 2 to help you.

External

Internal

Suppliers   Customers   Competitors

My organisation

Employees   Boss   Me

2 Now give a short talk to the other students in the class.

Communicating at work

Telephoning 2: Taking messages

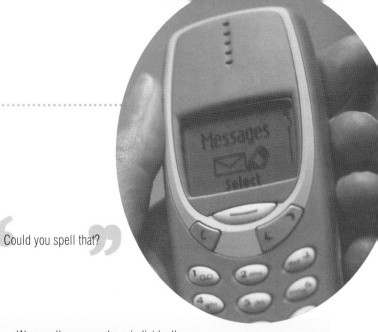

Could you spell that, please?

1 Work in pairs. Student A should look at page 104 and Student B at page 106.

2 Look at these questions:

> Could you repeat that?

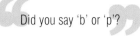
> Did you say 'b' or 'p'?

> Could you spell that?

Ask your partner for his/her address and write it down. Use the questions to help you.

Could I have your number? ▶▶ 5.1

1 Listen to the way we say these phone numbers:

678586   784367   488598   598889   584989

2 Repeat the numbers to your partner.

3 Say your office, mobile and home numbers to your partner.

> We usually say numbers individually.
> People in the UK say 'oh'.
> People in the USA say 'zero'.
> 00 44 = the international code
> 01904 = the area/city code

Can I take a message?

1 Choose four of these sentences (a–h) to complete the phone conversation below.

a I'm afraid he's not in the office today.
b Could you ask him to call me back?
c He's not at his desk at the moment.
d Could you spell that, please?

e Can I take a message?
f Could I have your name and number?
g I'll make sure he gets the message.
h I'll call back later.

A: Hello.	B: Could I speak to Mr García?
A: I'm afraid he's in a meeting. (1)	B: (2) ....
A: Of course. (3)	B: Yes, my name's Fiala. That's F-i-a-l-a.
A: Did you say 'F'?	B: Yes, 'F'. Fiala.
A: OK, so that's F-i-a-l-a.	B: Yes. That's right. And my number is 7877545.
A: 787545.	B: No, 7877545.
A: Double 7 – 545. OK, Mr Fiala, (4)	B: Thank you. Goodbye.

2 Listen and check. ▶▶ 5.2

3 Practise reading the conversation with a partner.

4 Practise taking messages. Student A should look at page 104, and Student B at page 107.

> **Remember**
>
> When taking messages on the phone, remember to:
>
> • Ask for spelling: Could you spell that?
> • Check spelling: Did you say ... ?
> • Repeat information you hear: So that's ...

On the agenda

Speaking
Where you live

Social phrases
Shopping

Vocabulary
Location and shopping

" I really like living near where I work. "

I love living in the countryside.

Warm up

Read what people often say about where they live.
Do you think the same about where you live?

6 Downtown Barcelona

I like living near my family.

" I prefer to live close to good shops – I love shopping. "

Shopping

1 Complete the dialogues with phrases (a–j) below.

Looking around

A: Hello, (1) .... ?
B: No, it's OK thanks. (2) ....
A: OK. Just ask me if you need some help.

Asking for help

B: (3) .... , please?
A: Yes, of course. The changing rooms are just there.
B: Thank you.
A: (*A few minutes later*) So, how's that?
B: I'm not sure. (4) .... Have you got it in a larger size?
A: No, I'm sorry, we haven't.
B: Oh, I see. I think (5) ....

Asking about the price

B: Excuse me, (6) .... , please?
A: It's €47.
B: OK, I'll (7) ....
A: Fine. You can pay over there.

Asking about payment

A: That's €47, please.
B: Thank you. (8) .... ?
A: Yes, of course. (9) .... , please.
B: OK.
A: Here's your card and (10) .... Thank you.
B: Thank you. Goodbye.

a how much is this
b It's a bit small
c Sign here
d your receipt is in the bag
e I'll leave it then
f can I help you
g Can I pay by credit card
h I'm just looking
i Could I try this on
j take it

Have a go

Cover the dialogues above and make your own, starting with the words below.

Looking around
Hello ...

Asking about the price
Excuse me, ...

Asking for help
Could I try ...?

Asking about payment
That's ...

2 Now listen and check. ▶▶ 6.1

3 Practise reading the dialogues with a partner.

Listen to this

A shoppers' paradise

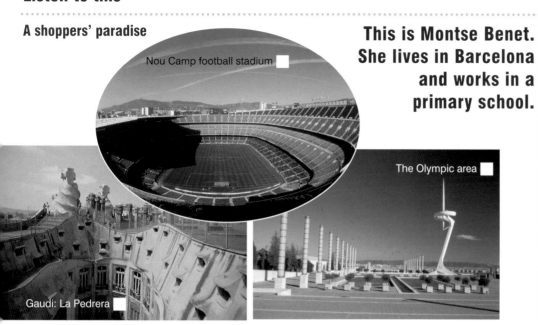

Nou Camp football stadium

This is Montse Benet. She lives in Barcelona and works in a primary school.

The Olympic area

Gaudi: La Pedrera

1 Listen to Montse talking about Barcelona and her love of shopping. Tick (✔) the pictures she talks about. ▶▶| 6.2

2 Listen again. Are these sentences true or false? ▶▶| 6.2

1 Montse lives outside the centre of Barcelona.   T   F

2 Montse lives 20 minutes' walk from the Gothic quarter.   T   F

3 Prices are very high in the Modernist quarter.   T   F

4 Montse's favourite shopping area is the Passeig de Gracia.   T   F

Hand-made gifts

Fine wines

> **What do you think?**   Would you like to live in Barcelona? Which things would you like to see and do?

Passeig de Gracia

Shopping in a department store

Fresh food

The words you need ... to talk about where you live

1 Choose the correct preposition in these sentences.

1 I live *in* / *on* the city centre.

2 I live *at* / *in* quite a small street.

3 I live *near* / *by* the main shopping centre.

4 I live *on* / *outside* Barcelona.

5 Sitges is *at* / *on* the coast.

6 Sitges is about 40 kilometres *for* / *from* Barcelona.

7 Sitges is a small town not far *of* / *from* Barcelona.

8 Barcelona is *in* / *at* the north-east of Spain.

Now listen and check. ▶▶| 6.3

Describe where you live with some similar sentences.

2 Montse and Samantha are talking about what to see around Barcelona. Complete the conversation with the verbs in the box. There is more than one possible answer for some of the gaps.

| takes | catch | go | get | walk |

SAMANTHA: So, let's plan the weekend. Can we go somewhere?

MONTSE: Yes, what about Sitges? It's a really nice place.

SAMANTHA: How far is it from Barcelona?

MONTSE: Not far. By bus, it (1) .... about 40 minutes. Or perhaps we could (2) .... by train.

SAMANTHA: I'd like to go by bus. Where do we (3) .... it?

MONTSE: The bus station is quite close – it will only take us about five minutes to (4) .... there.

SAMANTHA: Good! And I've got a friend who lives in Vilanova. Is it far from Sitges?

MONTSE: No, it's quite close. We can probably (5) .... there by bus. It's a lovely place.

Now listen and check ▶▶| 6.4

It's time to talk

A client is visiting your organisation and wants to know about your area. Talk about where you live and interesting places you can travel to locally. Take turns to play the client. Use the ideas below to help you.

<u>Where you live</u>

I live in ... (country)
I live near ...

<u>Places to see near where you live</u>

You can go to ...
It's in the north/south/east/west of ...
It's ... kilometres from ...

<u>Travelling to places near where you live</u>

You can get there by car/train.
It takes ... minutes/hours.
It's a ... minute/hour walk/drive/bus ride.

<u>What you think about the place</u>

It's nice.
It's lovely.
It's not very nice.

Is it far? How far away is it?

Remember

Learn these useful questions for travelling:

- Where is ... ?
- Is it far?
- How far away is it?
- Can you get there by bus/train/ ... ?
- How do you get there?

On the agenda

Speaking
Where you work

Grammar
There is/are …
Countable and uncountable nouns
Some and *any; a lot of*

Pronunciation
Linking

Meet Stein Idar Stokke. He is a manager for Telenor in Norway.

7 Changing workspace

Warm up

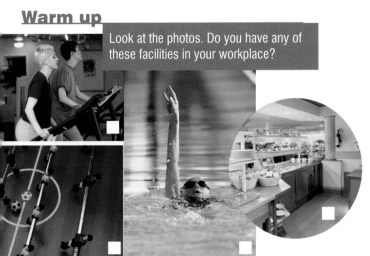

Look at the photos. Do you have any of these facilities in your workplace?

Listen to this

This is where I work

1 Listen to Stein talking about his workplace. Tick (✓) the photos showing facilities which are in his office building. ▶▶ **7.1**

2 Listen again and answer these questions. ▶▶ **7.1**
  1 How many people have a personal office?
  2 What do employees like about the new office?
  3 What does Stein like about the new office?
  4 What doesn't Stein like about the new office?

What do you think?   Would you like to work in an office like Stein's? Why? Why not?

Check your grammar

Countable and uncountable nouns with *There is … / There are …*

We can use *There is / There are* with countable nouns and uncountable nouns to describe where we work. Complete the sentences below using the words in the box.

| | any | | are | | some |
| | | are | | is | aren't |

	Countable singular	Countable plural	Uncountable nouns
Positive	There's a restaurant.	There (1) .... some	There's (2) ....
	There's an open office.	table games.	information on the new database.
Negative	There isn't a fixed desk.	There aren't (3)	There isn't any paper.
	There isn't an exercise room.	personal offices.	There's no paper.
	There's no solution.	There are no personal offices.	
Question	Is there a restaurant?	(4) .... there any	(5) .... there any
	Is there a swimming pool?	places to work in private?	personal space?
Answer	Yes, there is.	Yes, there are.	Yes, there is.
	No, there isn't.	No, there (6)	No, there isn't.

Note **1** We often use *some* in positives and *any* in negatives and questions. But we also use *some* when we ask for or offer something.

  Example   *Would you like some coffee?*

2 We can use *a lot of* in positives, negatives and questions with countable plural nouns and uncountable nouns.

  Examples   *There are a lot of table games.*
  There isn't a lot of time.

Grammar reference pages 113–114 ➡

Do it yourself

1 Correct the mistakes in these sentences.

 1 There is two training rooms on the first floor.
 2 There aren't any private office on the top floor.
 3 Is there a computer equipment on the first floor?
 4 There isn't a lot of spaces in the car park.

2 Bob is showing David round his office. Complete the dialogue with the correct question, negative or positive form of *There is* or *There are*.

DAVID: So, (1) .... a car park for employees?

BOB: Yes, (2) .... some space but only for top management.

DAVID: What do other people do?

BOB: Well, (3) .... a railway station nearby so lots of people come by train.

DAVID: I see. What about lunch? (4) .... a staff restaurant?

BOB: No, but (5) .... a lot of bars and restaurants in the same street.

DAVID: (6) .... a gym or swimming pool?

BOB: No, (7) .... anything like that. But (8) .... two parks across the street and a swimming pool half a kilometre away.

DAVID: (9) .... somewhere I can get a drink?

BOB: Yes, (10) .... a lot of drinks machines in the building. Let's get something.

Now listen and check. ▶▶|7.2

3 Choose the correct words in these sentences. Sometimes more than one word or phrase is possible.

1	There are	some / a lot of / any	new computers for everyone.
2	There's	some / any / no	information on our intranet.
3	There aren't	any / a lot of / no	free spaces in our car park.
4	There isn't	a / some / any	nice food in the staff restaurant.
5	There's	a lot of / any / no	new furniture in my office.

Make similar sentences about your workplace.

4 Ask your partner questions about his/her workplace. Find out three positive and three negative things, and write them down.

"Are there any …?"

"Is there any …?"

"Is there a …?"

"Are there a lot of …?"

Positive things		**Negative things**	
1		1	
2		2	
3		3	

Linking

> 5 vowels: a e i o u
> 21 consonants: b c d f g h j k l m n p q r s t v w x y z

1 Listen to three sentences. Which one sounds more natural? ▶▶|7.3

In normal speech, we usually connect final consonant sounds to following vowels. The arrows show where the words are linked.

Example: There are a lot of small cafés.

2 Listen to these sentences. Use arrows to link the connected sounds. ▶▶|7.4

1 Telenor is a big company.

2 It's a very big building.

3 I think it's very, very flexible.

4 There's a big fitness centre, which is very good.

5 Yes, I like it a lot.

Practise saying the sentences with the linked sounds.

It's time to talk

Your organisation is moving offices. You and your partner are looking at two possible locations. Student A should look at page 104 and Student B at page 107. Ask and answer questions about the two possible offices and make notes below.

Use questions and answers like these.

Student A: "Are there any individual offices?"

Student B: "Yes, there are. It's not open plan."

Student A: "Sounds good!"

	Office 1	Office 2
The building		
Individual offices		
Car park		
Staff restaurant		
Swimming pool		
Smoking room		
The area		
Railway station		
Shops		
Fitness centre		
Banks		
Restaurants		

Remember

When talking about places, remember to:

- Use *There is/are* ... : There's a big car park.

- Ask questions with *Is/Are there* ... : Is there a staff restaurant?

Now decide which location is best for you.

On the agenda

Speaking
The people you work with

Communicating at work
Describing people at work

Vocabulary
Meeting a visitor at the airport

This is Shirley Fagan. She works for an advertising agency in Australia. Meet her and her A team, the group of people she works with.

8 The A team

Warm up

Which sentences describe you? Compare yourself with your partner.

"I'm always on time."

"I'm a hard worker."

"I'm well organised."

"I often feel stressed."

"I'm often late."

"I'm a bit lazy sometimes."

"I'm a bit disorganised."

"I'm usually very relaxed."

Read on

We're a great team

1 We interviewed Shirley Fagan about the people she works with. Match the people in Shirley's team with one of her descriptions.

1 My manager
2 My favourite colleague
3 My customer
4 My husband
5 My PA

A All managers need a good assistant and Jack is fantastic. He's very good at organising things, very efficient, friendly and positive. He smiles all the time and always has a lot of energy.

B Jean is from Paris and he's my boss. He's a great motivator – he gives me a lot of support and always tells me when I do a good job. One thing I don't like about him is that he's always ten minutes late for meetings.

C John is the financial man in the team. He's a special character, good at his job, but some people don't like him because he can be very direct. Most people think he's rude. He's my husband but working together isn't a problem for us.

D David's based in Darwin. He buys a lot from us but when we discuss prices he can be very aggressive and impatient. Sometimes I have to say 'no'. You can't always say 'yes' to your clients.

E Katie is nice. She's a sales manager, responsible for New South Wales. She's very confident and so is excellent at presenting to customers. She's also very creative – she loves thinking about new products. We get on really well together, both in and outside the office.

2 Read the text again and match a person in Shirley's team with these sentences.

1 This person is not very popular with some colleagues. ....

2 This person is difficult to do business with. ....

3 This person has a lot of new ideas. ....

4 This person is not very punctual for meetings. ....

5 This person is very well organised. ....

Jack

Shirley

What do you think? Who are the two most important people in your working life? Why?

The words you need ... to describe people

1 Complete these sentences with a word from the box. You can use a dictionary to help you.

1 I can do my job quickly and well. I'm very *efficient*.

2 I always have a lot of new ideas. I'm very ....

3 I hate waiting for anything. I'm very ....

4 I want to be the best! I'm very ....

5 I say what I think. I'm very ....

6 I always arrive for meetings on time. I'm very ....

7 I'm not afraid to speak English! I'm very ....

direct

impatient

punctual

~~efficient~~

competitive

confident

creative

Jean

Make sentences about people you know.

your boss	your customer	your neighbour
your children/parents	your partner	your teacher

Example: My boss is very creative.

Katie

David

2 Look at two important ways to build sentences using quality adjectives.

She's <u>good</u> at presenting. = the verb *to be* + <u>adjective</u> + *at* + **activity**
She's an <u>excellent</u> tennis player. = the verb *to be* + *a/an* + <u>adjective</u> + **personal noun**

Use the table below to make sentences about yourself. Can you add one or two of your own ideas?

Activity		Personal noun		Quality adjectives
Business	General	Business	General	excellent/great
presenting	socialising	presenter	socialiser	very good
managing people	football	manager	footballer	good
selling	tennis	sales person	tennis player	not very good
(your ideas)	(your ideas)	(your ideas)	(your ideas)	bad
				very bad
				terrible/awful

Example: I'm great at presenting but not very good at making coffee!

It's time to talk

Describe a person you know. Don't say the name of the person or their job. Can the other people in class guess who you are describing? Talk about the following:

- Age
- Job and responsibilities
- Free-time interests

- Two positive qualities
- Two negative qualities
- One quality of the person which is similar to you.

Communicating at work

Meeting a visitor at the airport

1 Koji is a Japanese client of Shirley's. He plans to visit Perth to see her and confirms his visit by email. Complete the email using the words in the box.

take

flight   meet

seeing   confirm

wishes   arrival

plan

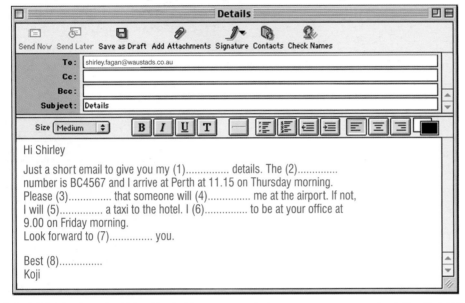

Send Now	Send Later	Save as Draft Add Attachments Signature Contacts Check Names

To: shirley.fagan@waustads.co.au
Cc:
Bcc:
Subject: Details

Size [Medium] **B** *I* U T

Hi Shirley

Just a short email to give you my (1).............. details. The (2)..............
number is BC4567 and I arrive at Perth at 11.15 on Thursday morning.
Please (3)............... that someone will (4)............... me at the airport. If not,
I will (5)............... a taxi to the hotel. I (6)............... to be at your office at
9.00 on Friday morning.
Look forward to (7)............... you.

Best (8)...............
Koji

2 Shirley meets Koji at the airport. Listen and tick (✔) the sentences you hear. ▶▶8.1

It's good to see you again. How are you? ☐   No, I can manage, thanks. ☐

Did you have a good trip? ☐   OK. Here we are. ☐

Can I help you with your luggage? ☐   The car's in the car park. ☐

At home it's cold and wet. ☐   How's the weather back home? ☐

3 You are meeting an important client at the airport. Use the ideas below to role-play the meeting with your partner. Then change roles.

How to welcome a visitor

Hello. It's good to ...   How's the ...?

Greet →	**Ask about the trip** →	**Tell your visitor about the car** →	**Offer to help with their luggage** →	**Ask about the weather back home**
	✈			

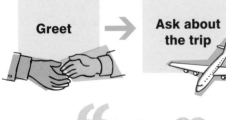

Did you have ...?   The car is ...   Can I ...?

Remember

When welcoming visitors, remember to:
- Welcome positively: Welcome to ...
- Ask polite questions: Is this your first time ... ?
- Offer help if they need it: Let me help you with ...

Continue with your own ideas.

On the agenda

Speaking
Where you live

Social phrases
Getting around

Vocabulary
City life

9 I love Chicago

Warm up

What is your favourite city? Is there a city you really don't like?
Which city do you really want to visit?

Getting around

1 Complete the dialogues with phrases (a–h) below.

Buying a ticket

A: Hi. Three tickets for the Wendella Lake tour, please. (1) ....
B: That's $22.50, please.
A: Thanks. (2) .... leave, please?
B: At 3 o'clock, in 25 minutes.
A: OK. Thanks.

Taking the train

A: Excuse me. (3) .... ?
B: No. You need to take the blue line.
A: OK, so where do I go?
B: Go to Lake Street and transfer to the blue line and then
(4) ....
A: Great. Thanks for your help.

Catching a bus

A: Excuse me. (5) .... the Magnificent Mile from here?
B: Yes, you want a number 151 or a 147. Or you can take a cab or walk.
A: (6) .... ?
B: Ten minutes. But they're not always on time.
A: Thanks.

Getting a cab

A: How much is that?
B: That's $10.20.
A: Here you are, $12.00. (7) ....
B: Thank you.
A: (8) .... ?
B: Sure. Here you go. Have a good day.

a	Could I have a receipt	**e**	Two adults and one child
b	What time does the next ferry	**f**	take it to the end of the line
c	Keep the change	**g**	Does this go to O'Hare Airport
d	When's the next bus	**h**	Can I get a bus to

Have a go

Cover the dialogues above and make your own, starting with the words below.

Buying a ticket

Hi ...

Taking the train

Excuse me. Does this go to ... ?

Catching a bus

Excuse me. Can I ... ?

Getting a cab

How much ...

2 Now listen and check. ▶▶|9.1

3 Practise reading the dialogues with a partner.

Listen to this

It's my kind of town

1 Listen to Ellen talking about Chicago. Tick (✔) the pictures she talks about. ▶▶|9.2

Meet Ellen Zlotnick, who lives in Chicago. She will introduce you to the city.

| A Lebanese restaurant

| The Sears Tower

| Louis Armstrong

| The Chicago Cubs

| The Taste of Chicago

| Muhammad Ali

| Al Capone

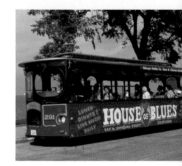

| The Chicago tram system

2 Listen again. Are these sentences true or false? ▶▶|9.2

1 Chicago has the oldest skyscraper in America. T ☐ F ☐
2 Chicago has the tallest building in the world. T ☐ F ☐
3 There are four million visitors to The Taste of Chicago. T ☐ F ☐
4 The first McDonald's restaurant was established in Chicago. T ☐ F ☐

What do you think? Would you like to visit Chicago? Which things would you like to see and do?

The words you need ... to talk about city life

1 Look at the things you can go to or see in a big city. Match the words and pictures.

1 a statue	☐	6 a bridge	☐
2 an art gallery	☐	7 a lake	☐
3 a castle	☐	8 a church	☐
4 a square	☐	9 a skyscraper	☐
5 a theatre	☐	10 a mosque	☐

Which of these things do you have in your town or city?

2 Look at the adjectives in these sentences and match
them with their opposites in the box.

1 The restaurants are very busy.
2 The streets are very safe at night.
3 The lakeside beach is very clean.
4 The city centre is very noisy.
5 Temperatures are very high in summer.
6 You need warm clothes in the spring.
7 Public transport is awful.
8 The city is beautiful at night.
9 The nightclubs are always full.

cool	dirty	quiet
low	ugly	excellent
dangerous	empty	quiet

Make sentences with the adjectives about where you live.

Example: Where I live, the public transport is excellent.

It's time to talk

A very important customer is visiting your organisation
and wants to find out about where you live. Your partner
is the visitor and will ask you questions about the things
he/she can see and do. The person playing the visitor
should make notes about what you say.

Examples for a visitor to Prague:

Is Prague warm in the summer?   *Yes, really warm. It's too hot!*

Are there a lot of things to do?   *Yes, sure. You can …*

You can walk across Charles Bridge in Prague.

Activities	Visitor notes
Things to see	
Things to do	
The weather	
The nightlife	
Restaurants	
Public transport	
Other ideas	

Now change roles.

On the agenda

Speaking
Comparing

Grammar
Comparative and
superlative adjectives

Pronunciation
Weak stress 1

Ablaziz Esseid travels 30 weeks a year in his job as a trader for Total. Here he talks about the different foods he eats around the world.

10 Eating around the world

Warm up

Match the foods and countries.
What kind of food do you prefer? Why?

Morocco	curry
India	roast beef and Yorkshire pudding
England	burritos
Mexico	foie gras
France	couscous

Listen to this

Favourite food

1 Listen to Ablaziz talking about the food he eats when he travels on business. Which of the above countries does he talk about? ▶▶|10.1

2 Listen again. Are these sentences true or false? ▶▶|10.1

1 English food is heavier than French food. T ☐ F ☐

2 London restaurants are more expensive than restaurants in Paris. T ☐ F ☐

3 Jordanian food is better than most European food. T ☐ F ☐

4 Restaurants are the best place to discuss business. T ☐ F ☐

What do you think? Ablaziz says: '... for me, eating good food is one of the most important things in life.' Do you agree with Ablaziz?

Check your grammar

Comparative and superlative adjectives
We can compare things using the comparative and superlative forms of adjectives. Complete the table below.

Rule	Adjective	Comparative	Superlative
One syllable: add -er/-est	cheap	(1)	cheapest
Two syllables ending in y: change y to i and add -er/-est	tasty	(2)	(3) ....
Most other two syllable adjectives*: use more/less and most/least	modern	more/less modern	(4) .... /least modern
Three or more syllables: use more/less and most/least	expensive	(5) .... /less expensive	most/(6) .... expensive
Learn the irregular adjectives!	good (8)	better worse	(7) .... worst
*Some two syllable adjectives take -er/-est. Some can take both forms.	quiet polite polite	quieter politer more/less polite	quietest politest more/least polite
If you are not sure, use a dictionary.			*Grammar reference page 114*

Do it yourself

1 Now correct the mistakes in these sentences.

  1 I learn vocabulary more fast than I learn grammar.

  2 For me, English grammar is more easier than French grammar.

  3 My Spanish is badder than my French.

  4 The importantest language for international business is English.

Walking is sometimes faster than travelling by car!

2 Put the words in order to make sentences.

1	than	healthier	fresh fruit	chocolate	is
2	cheaper	salmon	than	is	Russian caviar
3	than	Champagne	is	Cava	more expensive
4	is	quicker to eat	a meal in a restaurant	a sandwich	than
5	English food	is	spicier	than	Indian food

Now listen and check. ▶▶|10.2

Test your partner Ask him/her to make comparative sentences by pointing at the ideas in the box.

French food / Greek food	New York / Prague
Gucci clothes / Marks & Spencer clothes	
Air travel / rail travel	Chinese / English

3 Read this extract from a London restaurant guide and correct the mistakes in the sentences below.

Eating out

	Cuisine	Food quality	Price (three courses)	Size
Chez Pierre	French	★	£30	70m²
Gianni's	Italian	★★	£45	80m²
The Mogul	Indian	★★★	£50	55m²
The Knightsbridge	English	★★★★	£60	65m²

1 The Knightsbridge is less expensive than Chez Pierre.
2 Gianni's is the smallest restaurant in the guide.
3 The Mogul is bigger than Gianni's.
4 Chez Pierre is the most expensive restaurant in the guide.
5 The Knightsbridge has the worst food in the guide.

Test your partner Make sentences about the restaurants. Your partner must say if they are right or wrong without looking at the book.

Example: YOU: Gianni's is cheaper than Chez Pierre.

  PARTNER: That's wrong! Gianni's is more expensive.

Weak stress 1

1 Listen to the pronunciation of these two sentences. How do we pronounce the underlined syllables and words? ▶▶|10.3

The Pentium 3 processor is cheaper than the Pentium 4.

Bordeaux wines are amongst the most famous wines in the world.

We pronounce some words and syllables with strong stress, others with weak stress. All the underlined words and syllables have weak stress. We use /ə/ to make these sounds. We call this 'the schwa' /ə/.

2 Listen and underline the weak stress in these sentences from an airline advertisement. Then practise saying the sentences aloud. ▶▶|10.4

3 How does your organisation compare with its competitors? Write down some similar sentences about your organisation. Underline the weak stress and practise saying them to your partner.

Five reasons to fly with us!

1. **Polite?** *We're politer than the rest.*
2. **Fast?** *We're faster than the rest.*
3. **Cheap?** *We're less expensive than the rest.*
4. **Big?** *We're the biggest in the world.*
5. **Good?** *We're the best in the world.*

It's time to talk

You work on the social committee of your organisation. You want to plan a weekend break for the people in your department by choosing one of the three package holidays below. Student A should look at the file card on page 104, Student B at page 107 and Student C at page 109 (if you are in a group of three).

Rome

Average temperature 28°C

★★★★ Hotel (Navona)

Visit the Roman Forum, the Colosseum and St Peter's Basilica. Experience the great names of Italian fashion.

3 nights €695 pp. all inc.

Travel time 5 hours

London

Average temperature 20°C

★★★ Hotel (Victoria)

Visit Buckingham Palace, the British Museum and see a West End musical. Go shopping in Chelsea and Oxford Street.

2 nights €495 pp. all inc.

Travel time 2 hours

Paris

Average temperature 21°C

★★★★ Hotel (16th Arrondissement)

Visit the Eiffel Tower, the Louvre and see the beautiful buildings of Central Paris. Eat in a top Montparnasse restaurant.

3 nights €595 pp. all inc.

Travel time 4 hours

Remember

Use *than* after a comparative:
• London restaurants are *more expensive* than in Paris.

Use *the* before a superlative:
• Italian food is *the best* in the world.

Which one did you choose? Why?

On the agenda

Speaking
What you want from your job

Communicating at work
Emails 1: Giving your emails a clear structure

Vocabulary
Work

Meet Paul Munden. He runs an Internet service for people in education from his home in the UK. Find out what he likes about his job.

11 Nice work

Warm up

Tell your partner two things you like and one thing you don't like about your job. Use these ideas or your own ideas.

salary   colleagues   office
travel to work   food

I get a very high salary!

I get a very low salary!

Read on

Homeworking

1 We interviewed Paul Munden about his job. Match the headings with his answers.

1 Working with my wife   **2** Working with the Internet   **3** Working with writers   **4** Working and relaxing

I'm a writer myself, writing poetry. But I work for the National Association of Writers in Education. This is an organisation to help writers and teachers work together to give courses on writing in schools. In this way, we help children and adults write poetry or whatever they want. It's great. I love working in education and with writing.

The Internet is very important to my work. I work a lot with our website, where we put ideas which teachers and writers can use in their lessons. But for me, technology is a problem. I live in the country so I have a slow Internet connection and I often have connection problems. It's really frustrating sometimes.

Sometimes it's difficult to relax because my work is at home, but I never work at the weekend. We have a nice garden and I enjoy sitting there and doing some gardening. I also play football with friends. But you have to be careful because it's very easy to stay at home too much. So you must push yourself to go out and meet friends.

I spend a lot of time working from home, which is great. I prefer to work alone. I can get up in the morning and go directly to my desk with no traffic problems. Also, when the children were younger, it was nice to look after them. And now I work with my wife because she is the organisation's database manager. I like it because we can discuss work problems very easily and openly. But some people think spending all that time together is terrible.

2 Read the text again and find:

  1 two things Paul does to relax.
  2 what Paul likes about working from home.
  3 what Paul has problems with at work.
  4 what Paul likes about his job.

What do you think? What is similar and different in your job? Do you work at home? Would you like to? Why? Why not?

The words you need ... to talk about work

1 Complete these sentences with the correct word from the diagram.

1 On Tuesdays I work .... home.

2 I never work .... the weekend.

3 I usually work .... a team.

4 I want to work .... , maybe in China.

5 I often work .... and enjoy the quiet!

6 I work .... , not full-time.

In pairs, ask questions using these expressions.

Example:

"Do you sometimes work at home?"

"Yes, I do."

"Do you like working at home?"

"Not really."

2 Match the sentences with the cartoons.

1 I have too many meetings.

2 I have a very good boss.

3 I have a big office.

4 I work long hours.

5 I have too much to do.

6 I can socialise with colleagues a lot.

7 I travel a lot for work.

8 I can work from home twice a week.

a  b  c

Which sentences describe you?

d  e  f  g  h

It's time to talk

1 What do **you** want from your job? Number the following things in order of importance in the table below.

Job	You	Person 1	Person 2
A good salary Training A good manager Flexible working hours Travel opportunities Working from home Working in a team Good holidays Other			

So what's important to you?

For me a good boss is more important than money, and I have to like the people at work.

2 Now interview two other people and complete the table.

Communicating at work

Emails 1: Giving your emails a clear structure

1 When writing emails, we often write with four main parts: the greeting, the reason for writing, the action point and the close. Complete the email opposite with the phrases in the box.

   a   Best wishes
   b   Please could you send me an agenda as soon as possible?
   c   Dear Francisco
   d   I can confirm that I will be at the sales meeting next week.

```
From: Sandrine Gaslain
To: Francisco Ferreira
Subject: Sales meeting


Greeting              (1) ........
Reason for writing    (2) ........
Action point          (3) ........
Close                 (4) ........
```

2 Match the four reasons for writing with the action points.

Reasons for writing

1   I need to contact John Peters about a computer problem but can't find his number or email address.

2   It would be good to discuss the production schedule.

3   Attached is an Excel file with information about product no. 333.

4   I spoke to Pedro yesterday on the phone about our trip to Canada.

Action points

a   Can we discuss flight arrangements for Tuesday after the marketing meeting?
     See you

b   Could you send them to me asap?
     Thanks

c   Please contact me if you need any more information.
     Best regards

d   Could you give me a call tomorrow?
     Regards

3 Write three emails using the notes in your diary. Structure the emails carefully. Give a clear reason for writing and an action point.

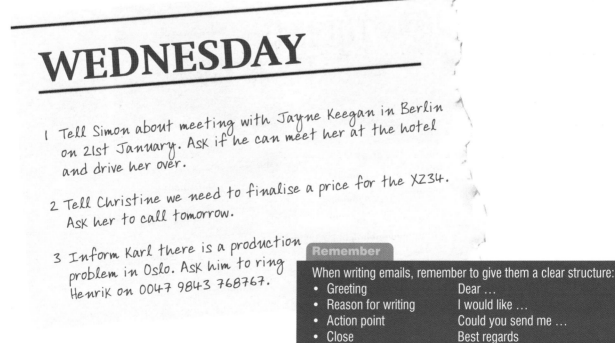

WEDNESDAY

1 Tell Simon about meeting with Jayne Keegan in Berlin on 21st January. Ask if he can meet her at the hotel and drive her over.

2 Tell Christine we need to finalise a price for the XZ34. Ask her to call tomorrow.

3 Inform Karl there is a production problem in Oslo. Ask him to ring Henrik on 0047 9843 768767.

Remember

When writing emails, remember to give them a clear structure:
- Greeting   Dear ...
- Reason for writing   I would like ...
- Action point   Could you send me ...
- Close   Best regards

Speaking
Sport and physical exercise

Social phrases
Responding to news

Vocabulary
Verbs and nouns for sport and physical activities

Warm up

Do you like sport? Or do you prefer watching it? Is there any physical exercise in your job?

12 Do you salsa?

I've got news for you

1 Complete the dialogues with phrases (a–h) below.

Responding to good news

A: Hi. Good weekend?
B: Yes, very. I have some news. My wife's pregnant.
A: Wonderful. (1) .... !
B: Thanks. We're very happy.
A: Oh, good. (2) ....

Responding to interesting news

A: Hey, Peter. I've got an email from China.
B: (3) .... ?
A: Yes, it's a new customer, I think. They want information about our products.
B: Great. Please tell me if you hear any more from them.
A: (4) ....

Responding to bad news

A: So you leave for the US tonight?
B: Don't ask! My trip's cancelled!
A: (5) .... ?
B: Because I have to stay here for a meeting with my boss.
A: Oh, well, (6) .... Now you can come to Helen's party tonight.

Responding to surprising news

A: See you tomorrow.
B: Yeah, see you. What are you doing tonight?
A: (7) .... I might go jogging.
B (8) .... ! I don't believe it. You hate sport.
A: Yes, but I need the exercise.

a	I'm not sure yet	**e** You're joking
b	Why's that	**f** never mind
c	Really	**g** Congratulations
d	We must celebrate	**h** Of course I will

2 Now listen and check. ▶▶12.1

3 Practise reading the dialogues with a partner.

Have a go

Cover the dialogues above and make your own, starting with the words below.

Good news

Hi. Good weekend?

Responding to interesting news

Hey ...

Responding to bad news

So ...

Responding to surprising new

See you tomorrow.

Listen to this

I hate watching TV

1 Listen to Ben, Alison and Roisin talking about sport and physical exercise. What are their main free-time activities? Write the initials by the activities (B, A, R). ▶▶|12.2

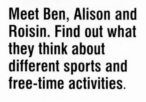

Meet Ben, Alison and Roisin. Find out what they think about different sports and free-time activities.

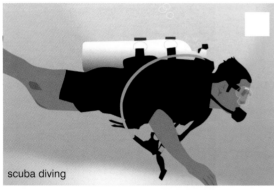

scuba diving

squash

motorcycle racing

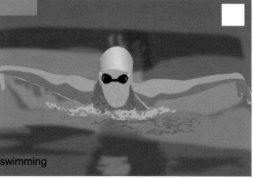

swimming

salsa dancing

tennis

flying

2 Now listen again. What do they say about their activities? Match a person to the sentences. Write their initials by the sentences (B, A, R). ▶▶|12.2

It's good exercise.

I have to relax after work.

Winning is not important.

I hate sport on TV.

I like being alone.

I like to socialise.

What do you think? 'People watch too much television. It's better to go out and do something!' Do you agree?

The words you need ... to talk about sport

1 Complete the sentences about famous sporting moments with the past form of the correct sports verb.

  1 In 2002 Germany .... to Brazil in the World Cup final.

  2 In the 2003 Wimbledon final, Serena Williams .... her sister, Venus.

  3 Michael Schumacher .... the 2001 Formula 1 Championship.

  4 In the 2002 Chicago marathon, Paula Radcliffe .... some of the best runners in the world.

  5 In the 1972 Olympics, Mark Spitz .... seven gold medals.

What's the difference between *win* and *beat*? Can you describe some more famous sporting moments using the verbs?

Verb	Past
win	won
lose	lost
play	played
beat	beat

Venus lost this one.

2 Which verbs go with these sports? Put each sport in the right column below. Sometimes the activity can go in more than one column.

Example: I go jogging = *go* + activity
     I do some / a little jogging = *do* + quantity + activity

running   yoga   aerobics   gymnastics   ice hockey   golf

cycling   football   swimming   walking   weight training   skiing

play	do	go
	some / a little jogging	jogging

Can you think of one or two more sports for each verb?

3 How do you say the following sporting scores?

Football
Real Madrid   0 – 0   Bayer Leverkusen
Real Madrid   1 – 0   Bayer Leverkusen
Real Madrid   1 – 1   Bayer Leverkusen
Real Madrid   2 – 1   Bayer Leverkusen

Tennis
Henri 15 – 0 Schmidt   Henri 30 – 15 Schmidt
Henri 15 – 15 Schmidt   Henri 40 – 40 Schmidt

4 In tennis, what is the difference between a *game*, a *set*, and a *match*?

It's time to talk

Ask other people in your group about sport and physical exercise. Make your own table like the one below, and complete it with information about what your partner likes and why he/she likes it. (If you don't like sport, tell your partner why not!)

	What	Why
Sports and activities you like doing		
Sports and activities you like to watch		
Sports and activities you dislike		
A sporting event you would like to see		
A sportsman or woman you like to watch		
Your favourite sport		
Your favourite sporting moment		

Remember

Learn verbs that go with sports:
  • play football   • do some yoga   • go skiing

On the agenda

Speaking
Your life and background

Grammar
The past simple

Pronunciation
Past simple verbs

Coco Chanel was one of the great designers and business figures of the 20th century.

Punk

Versace

Levis

13 Chanel

Warm up

Do you follow fashion? What kind of clothes do you like? Why?

Listen to this

Gabrielle (Coco) Chanel – inventor of the fashion industry

1 We interviewed fashion designer Julie Williams about Coco Chanel's life. Match the events in her life to the year they happened. ▶▶13.1

> 1883   1910   1921   1924   1946   1954   1971

a moved to Switzerland
b died at the age of 87
c opened her first clothes shop called 'Chanel Modes'
d joined with Pierre and Paul Wertheimer to create a company, Société des Parfums Chanel
e launch of the first perfume Chanel No. 5
f born in the Loire region of France
g returned to Paris

2 Listen again and answer the questions. ▶▶13.1

> 1 How did Coco get her name?
> 2 Why did she give her famous perfume the name Chanel No. 5?
> 3 What did Yves Saint Laurent do for her in 1967?
> 4 What can we see of Coco Chanel in the business world of today?

What do you think? 'She changed women's lives.' Is fashion important in your life?

Check your grammar

The past simple

We can use the past simple tense to talk about our past life and past events. Complete the sentences below.

<u>Question</u>
<u>The verb *to be*: was/were + noun/adjective</u>
How (1) .... the trip? (*noun*)
Were they happy? (*adjective*)

<u>Was/were + short answers</u>
Were you busy?
(4) .... they happy?

<u>Wh- questions</u>
When (5) .... you arrive?

<u>Did + short answers</u>
Did you have a good trip?

<u>Positive</u>

It was good.
They were very happy.

Yes, I was.
Yes, they were.

I (6) ....
yesterday.

Yes, I did.

<u>Negative</u>

It wasn't very interesting.
They (2) .... very happy.

No, I (3) ....
No, they weren't.

I (7) .... arrive today.

No, I didn't.

Irregular verbs
Write the correct forms.
do   did
get   (8) ....
go   (9) ....
have (10) ....

Irregular verbs

Irregular verbs do *not* form the past simple positive with the verb + *ed*.

Grammar reference page 115 ▶

Do it yourself

1 Correct the mistakes in these sentences.

    1 I have done it yesterday.
    2 I didn't had time.
    3 Did you were busy?
    4 What have you done last night?

2 Read about the life and career of Stella McCartney, a fashion designer today. Complete the following text with the correct form of the verbs in brackets.

1971   She (1) .... (be) born and grew up in England.

1986   At 15 she (2) .... (start) working with Christian Lacroix and spent several years apprenticed to a Savile Row tailor. She (3) .... (leave) because she (4) .... (not/want) to work with fur.

1995   She (5)................ (graduate) from London's Central St Martin's College of Art and Design.

1997   At 25, she (6) .... (join) Chloe and (7) .... (stay) there for four years.

2001   In March 2001 she (8) .... (leave) Chloe to begin her own label 'Stella McCartney' in partnership with Gucci. She (9) .... (launch) this label in Paris later that year. Her father and many celebrity friends (10) .... (be) there to support her.

3 Complete the questions about Stella McCartney's life. The answers are on the right to help you.

Questions	Answers
When (1) .... she born?	1971
Where did she (2) .... up?	England
Where (3) .... she (4) ....?	St Martin's College
When did she (5) .... Chloe?	In 1997
How (6) .... did she (7) .... there?	For four years

Ask your partner questions about his/her life and career.

4 The past simple is very important in everyday social conversation. Complete the dialogue.

GENEVIEVE: Afternoon, Peter. You look tired! What did you (1) .... last night?

PETER: Hi, I (2) .... to a restaurant for an early dinner and then to the cinema.

GENEVIEVE: What (3) .... you see?

PETER: A Russian film. It (4) .... about a family in Moscow. I don't remember the title.

GENEVIEVE: Was it good?

PETER: No, it (5) .... I (6) .... understand it really.

Now listen and check. ▶▶|13.2

Stella McCartney celebrates.

The past simple

1 Listen to the three different ways we pronounce *-ed*. ▶▶13.3

| /ɪd/ wanted | /t/ walked | /d/ played |

A simple rule: We only say /ɪd/ with verbs ending with the letters *t* or *d*.

2 Listen to the pronunciation of the verbs below. Decide if they are /t/ , /d/ or /ɪd/. ▶▶13.4

liked	wanted	received
decreased	increased	listened
decided	enjoyed	walked
looked	talked	visited

Test your partner Test your partner's pronunciation of regular verbs in the past tense. Point to a past verb. Your partner must say the word. Does he/she say the *-ed* ending correctly?

3 Pronounce the past form of these irregular verbs.

bring – brought	say – said	take – took
buy – bought	see – saw	tell – told
read – read	speak – spoke	think – thought

Now listen and check. ▶▶13.5

It's time to talk

Find out about your partner's past. How many questions can you ask about each subject below? There are some examples of questions to help you.

<u>Last night</u>

What did you do last night?
Did you ... ?

<u>Last weekend</u>

What did you do last weekend?
Did you ... ?

<u>The last music concert you went to</u>
Who did you see?
When did you ...?

<u>Your last holiday</u>
Where was your last holiday?
When did you ... ?

<u>Your first job</u>

What was your first job?
Did you like ... ?

Did you like your first job?

> **Remember**
>
> We use the past simple to make small talk:
>
> - What did you do last night?
> - How was the weekend?
> - Did you have a nice trip?

On the agenda

Speaking
Your organisation

Communicating at work
Welcoming visitors to your organisation

Vocabulary
Organisational structure

Meet Polly from Médecins Sans Frontières, an organisation of doctors and nurses helping people around the world.

14 Médecins Sans Frontières

Warm up

Which of these organisations do you know? What do they do?

MÉDECINS SANS FRONTIERES
ARTSEN ZONDER GRENZEN

Plan
Be a part of it.

WWF

Oxfam

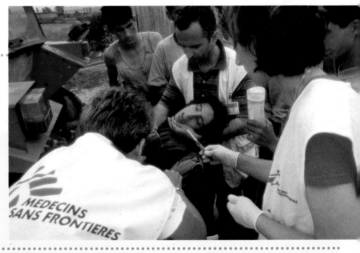

Read on

Médecins Sans Frontières – working to help people

1 We interviewed Polly Markandya about Médecins Sans Frontières. Match our questions with Polly's answers.

1 What do you do exactly?

2 What is Médecins Sans Frontières?

3 How is it organised?

4 Can you tell me about the history of Médecins Sans Frontières?

A It's a private organisation which gives medical help to people all over the world. Our philosophy is to help so we often work with people who are in a war situation. Or maybe there is a natural disaster like the food problem in Ethiopia in the 1980s.

B Médecins Sans Frontières was started just over 30 years ago by doctors working in Bangladesh and Nigeria. They wanted to give people in wars fast medical help. And these doctors wanted to tell the world about the terrible things they could see. This is the other part of the philosophy of Médicins Sans Frontières – to inform the world.

C At the beginning it was a French organisation, based in Paris. Now we work in 85 countries and plan our projects from three centres: Brussels, Paris and Barcelona, which handles many of our Latin American projects. The organisation is very decentralised and so needs people with a lot of energy to make it work.

D I'm a press officer and work in the communications department of Médecins Sans Frontières in London. Half my job is writing. I'm responsible for external and internal reports, but I also work with colleagues to communicate about medicine to the people in India and Africa. And I like that because I know the information I give is very important.

2 Read the text again and answer these questions.

 1 When was Médecins Sans Frontières started?
 2 What is the main activity of Médecins Sans Frontières?
 3 Where is Médecins Sans Frontières located?
 4 What does Polly like about her job in the organisation?

What do you think? Would you like to work for an organisation like Médecins Sans Frontières?

The words you need ... to talk about your organisation

1 Complete the sentences with the words from the box.

Organisation profile

 1 Médecins Sans Frontières was .... over 30 years ago.

 2 At the beginning, the .... was in Paris.

 3 We are now .... in Barcelona, Brussels and Paris.

 4 We are very international and have .... all over the world.

 5 We are .... in 85 countries.

 6 I work in the human resources ....

| headquarters |
| offices |
| department |
| based |
| started |
| active |

Make similar sentences about your organisation.

2 Complete the sentences about organisation activities with the correct verb.

Organisation activity

 1 Médecins Sans Frontières .... medical help in over 85 countries.

 2 Cambridge University Press .... a range of academic, educational and reference books.

 3 Ericsson .... equipment to the telecoms industry.

 4 Honda .... automobiles.

 5 Tesco .... millions of products in thousands of stores.

 6 Credit Suisse .... a wide range of banking services.

| makes |
| sells |
| provides |
| supplies |
| publishes |
| gives |

Make similar sentences about your organisation's activities.

MÉDECINS SANS FRONTIERES
ARTSEN ZONDER GRENZEN

HONDA
The Power of Dreams

TESCO

ERICSSON

It's time to talk

You want to find out about your partner's organisation. Student A should look at page 105 and Student B at page 107.

	Student A's organisation	Student B's organisation
Name		
When started		
Head office		
Locations		
Main activities		
Other information		

Communicating at work

Visiting an organisation

1 Use the words in the list to complete the conversation between Keiko Sumi and a company receptionist at the London office of a major charity.

<u>At reception</u>

KEIKO: Good morning. My name's Keiko Sumi. I've got an (1) .... with Patrick Hart at 10 o'clock.

RECEPTIONIST: Just a moment, Ms Sumi. I'll (2) .... him you're here. Could you (3) .... the visitors' book?

KEIKO: Of (4) ....

RECEPTIONIST: Right. Mr Hart will be with you in a (5) ....

KEIKO: Thank you.

RECEPTIONIST: And (6) .... you put on this security (7) .... , please?

moment
could
appointment
tell
course
badge
sign

2 Now listen and check your answers. ▶▶14.1

3 Practise reading the conversation with a partner.

4 Patrick Hart welcomes Keiko in reception and takes her to his office. Which of these sentences do you hear? ▶▶14.2

<u>At the office</u>

Nice to meet you. ▢	Please take a seat. ▢
Please follow me. ▢	Can I get you a drink? ▢
Is this your first trip to London? ▢	I hope you have a nice stay. ▢
Here we are. ▢	250 people work in this building. ▢
Did you find us OK? ▢	I'd love some tea. ▢

Welcoming visitors

5 You are meeting a visitor in the reception area of your organisation. Use the ideas below to role-play the meeting with your partner. Then change roles.

Remember

When meeting people who are visiting your organisation, remember to make them feel welcome:

- Welcome to …
- Please follow me.
- Please take a seat.
- Would you like something to drink?
- I hope you have a nice stay.

Welcoming visitors to your organisation

1 Greet → 2 Explain location of office

"There are … people … in this building."

"Please follow me …"

3 Say something about the office

"Here we are. Would you like …?"

"Nice to meet …"

"Is this your first visit …?"

4 Ask about visit → 5 Arrive at office – offer a drink → Can you continue with your own ideas?

On the agenda

Speaking
Holidays

Social phrases
Air travel

Vocabulary
Holidays and travel

Warm up

What kind of holidays do you like?
Do you like flying? Why? Why not?

15 Trekking in Nepal

Getting there

1 Complete the dialogues with phrases (a–j) below.

Checking in

A: (1) .... for Vienna?
B: Yes. Can I see your passport and ticket, please?
A: Of course.
B: Would you prefer a window or an aisle seat?
A: (2) .... , please.
B: (3) .... at gate 45.

Getting information at the gate

A: Excuse me, (4) .... about the Amsterdam flight?
B: Yes, the flight is delayed by 45 minutes.
A: OK, so (5) .... ?
B: Boarding is now at 18.30. (6) ....

On the plane

A: Excuse me, could you put your bag in the overhead locker?
B: They're full. (7) ....
A: Can you put it under your seat?
B: OK, (8) ....
A: Thank you.

Arriving without luggage

A: Hello, (9) ....
B: Right, I need some information from you.
A: OK, (10) .... and a local address.
B: Thank you. You're very organised.
A: Yes, this isn't the first time!

a my suitcase didn't arrive

b There's no room

c Can I check in here

d when is boarding

e An aisle seat

f do you have any information

g this is my flight information

h I'm very sorry for the delay

i I'll do that

j Boarding is at 17.30

Have a go

Cover the dialogues above and make your own, starting with the words below.

Checking in

Can I check in ...

Getting information at the gate

Excuse me, ...

On the plane

Excuse me, ...

Arriving without luggage

Hello, ...

2 Now listen and check. ▶▶|15.1

3 Practise reading the dialogues with a partner.

Listen to this

Walking at 5,000 metres

1 Listen to Jürgen talking about his holiday trekking in Nepal. Choose the correct information. ▶▶15.2

When?	5		10		15		years ago
Number of days walking	15		20		25		days
Distance walked every day	15		18		25		kilometres
Size of trekking group	2		15		20		people

2 Now listen again and answer these questions. ▶▶15.2

1 What problem did he have sometimes?
2 What equipment did he take?
3 What did he eat?
4 What did Jürgen enjoy most about the holiday?

What do you think? Would you like to go trekking in Nepal? Why? Why not?

Jürgen Robbert is from Germany and works as an IT trainer. Here he talks about his favourite holiday.

The words you need ... for holidays and travel

1 Complete these sentences about a holiday island with a verb from the box.

Things you can do

1 .... some sightseeing and a little walking.

2 .... to one of our great museums.

3 .... on the beach and sunbathe.

4 .... a car and explore the island.

5 .... and enjoy a great meal in one of our excellent restaurants.

6 .... photos of the wonderful places on the island.

Sit	Hire	Take	Do	Relax	Go

What do you like to do when you go on holiday?

2 Test your travel vocabulary by choosing the correct word in each sentence.

1 We went .... car.

2 We .... a bus.

3 Our plane was ten minutes ....

4 The taxi .... is just outside the airport.

5 I need a .... for my suitcases.

6 The flight .... will serve you coffee.

7 My holiday started badly. I .... my flight.

8 My .... is at 14.00.

Check your answers with a partner.

> in / by
> took / went
> late / latest
> station / rank
> trolley / bag
> man / attendant
> missed / lost
> fly / flight

My holiday started badly.

It's time to talk

1 Complete the table below with short notes about a holiday you once had.

2 Prepare some questions to ask two other people. Use Tapescript 15.2 on page 127 to help you.

A GREAT HOLIDAY!	YOU	PERSON 1	PERSON 2
Place			
Time			
Journey			
Accommodation			
Activities: 1 2 3			
Weather			
Best thing			
Worst thing			

3 Now interview the people and complete the table.

> **Remember**
>
> Travel questions can be very important for making conversation:
>
> • Where did you go on holiday?
> • Where did you stay?
> • How was the weather?
> • Did you have a good time?

Revision 1 Units 1–15

Grammar

1 Put the words in the correct order to make questions. Use the answers to help you.

1 do What do you?

        I'm a project manager.

2 do company you work Which for?

        I work for JETCON.

3 does come she Where from?

        She's from India.

4 the sport at you Do much weekend do?

        Well, I play a little golf.

5 you did do night What last?

        I went to the theatre.

6 have did to you What eat?

        I had salmon.

7 good you trip Did a have?

        Yes, I did.

8 take long it get here did How to?

        It took about three hours.

2 Correct the mistakes.

1 Is there a lot of restaurants near your office?
2 Is there a lot of informations on your website?
3 Is there a lot of people who need English for their job?
4 I think English grammar is more easier than Russian grammar.
5 Gucci clothes are generally expensiver than clothes from Marks & Spencer.
6 I think the weather today is more bad than yesterday.

General vocabulary

1 Match the opposites.

quiet	full
clean	ugly
empty	high
safe	noisy
beautiful	dirty
low	dangerous

2 Complete the sentences with the correct verb from the box.

play	relax	go	get	do	drive

1 I just want to sit on the beach and ....
2 I'd like to .... a little walking.
3 I'd prefer to .... swimming.
4 Is it possible to .... football somewhere?
5 I want to .... a bus and travel to the coast.
6 We have a car so let's .... somewhere.

Business communication

1 Choose the correct word to complete the telephone conversation.

PA: Taylors. Good morning.

JACK: Good morning. Could I (1) *speak/tell* to Paula Harker, please?

PA: Of course. (2) *Who/Who's* calling, please?

JACK: My name is Jack Meadows.

PA: Just a moment, I'll (3) *put/pass* you through.

JACK: Thanks.

PAULA: Jack. How are you?

JACK: Fine, thanks. And you?

PAULA: Not bad. Good to hear from you. How (4) *can/do* I help?

JACK: I'm just (5) *call/calling* to confirm the meeting tomorrow.

PAULA: Great. We need to discuss the budget for next year. So, see you at three?

JACK: Yes, three in my office.

PAULA: (6) *See/Talk* you tomorrow. Bye.

JACK: Bye.

2 Complete each missing word in the email.

(1) D................ Anneli
Please could you (2) s................... me a copy of your budget for next month? I need it for a meeting tomorrow. (3) A .... is a file with the agenda for the meeting. Please confirm you can open it.
If you need any more (4) i................ about tomorrow's meeting, feel free to (5) c................... me.
(6) B..................... regards

Pronunciation

1 Use arrows to link the connected sounds.

1 We have a message for you.
2 It's about our company.
3 It's a great place to work.
4 We need another 50 people.
5 So come and join us.

Now listen and check. ▶▶R1.1

2 Is the pronunciation of the endings of these verbs /t/, /d/ or /ɪd/? Put them in the correct column.

	/t/	/d/	/ɪd/
played			
needed			
liked			
decreased			
decided			
looked			
enjoyed			
listened			
walked			
visited			

Now listen and check. ▶▶R1.2

Business vocabulary

1 Complete the company profile with the correct word from the box.

headquarters	started	industry
responsible	based	offices

JETCON is an international company with (1) .... all over the world. It supplies equipment to the telecoms (2) .... Peter Jacobs, the CEO, (3) .... JETCON on his own in 1992. At first, his (4) .... was his bedroom. Now he is (5) .... in an exclusive building in the heart of London and is (6) .... for 3,150 staff.

2 Put the letters in the correct order.

1 This is the most important person for any company.

rostemuc ....

2 A person or organisation that gives you a job.

prelmoey ....

3 An organisation selling the same kinds of products as you.

premotitoc ....

4 Another word for worker.

peemoley ....

5 An organisation which sells you something so you can do your business.

slipperu ....

6 An expert, often external, which companies use.

stoutclann ....

Social phrases

1 Match the questions (1–6) with the correct response (a–f).
1 Can I pay by credit card?
2 When is boarding?
3 Last week we got an order for $10 million.
4 Is this your first time in the US?
5 Did you have a good trip?
6 Could you put it in the overhead locker?

a Congratulations.
b It was fine, thanks.
c Yes, it is.
d Of course. No problem.
e I'm afraid the flight is delayed.
f I'm sorry but it's full.

2 What do you say in these situations? Complete the sentences.

1 You see a colleague when you arrive at work.

How .... ?

2 You want a receipt in a restaurant.

Could .... ?

3 Ask if someone wants coffee.

Would .... ?

4 Tell the taxi driver you don't want any change.

Keep ....

5 Ask the price of something in a shop.

How .... ?

6 You say goodbye to a colleague on Friday evening.

Have ....

On the agenda

Speaking
Describing temporary situations

Grammar
The present continuous 1

Pronunciation
Sentence stress

Riggert Andersson is a project manager for the Swedish Railroad Authority working on a major construction project.

16 Project Stockholm

Warm up

What are you working on at the moment? Are you working on a special project? Are you enjoying working on it?

Listen to this

What project are you working on at the moment?

1 Listen to Riggert Andersson. Which is the correct information for his project report? ▶▶16.1

2 Listen again. Are these sentences true or false? ▶▶16.1

  1 People are working on the foundations at the moment.   T ☐ F ☐

  2 Riggert isn't enjoying the project.   T ☐ F ☐

  3 Riggert is working a lot with local people.   T ☐ F ☐

  4 Riggert is speaking a lot of English at work. T ☐ F ☐

Number of workers	
Around 200	☐
Over 500	☐
Location	
Stockholm city centre	☐
10 km outside Stockholm	☐
Architect	
Norman Foster	☐
Johan Briggs	☐
Project	
Building a new bridge	☐
Rebuilding an old bridge	☐

What do you think? Riggert says: 'When you build anything in Sweden, it's very important to think about the environment.' Is it the same in your country?

The present continuous 1

We can use the present continuous tense in three important ways to talk about temporary situations, with the focus on the present moment.

1 At the moment   I'm enjoying the lesson.

2 Current projects/situations   We're building a bridge in Stockholm.

3 Current changes/developments   The number of foreign visitors is increasing.

Complete the questions and answers.

Question	Positive	Negative
Where (1) .... you working?	I'm (2) .... from home today.	I'm (3) .... working in the office today.
Where (4) .... he staying?	He's staying at the Marriott Hotel.	He isn't (5) .... at the Swan Hotel.
How's the project going?	The project (6) .... going badly.	We (7) .... meeting our targets.

Questions + short answers

1 Are they speaking English?	Yes, they are.	No, they're (8) ....
2 Are you enjoying the project?	Yes, I (9)	No, I'm (10) ....
3 Is business increasing?	Yes, it is.	No, it isn't. / No, it's not.

Note: The present continuous is also used to talk about fixed future plans. See Unit 25.   *Grammar reference pages 116–117* ➡

Do it yourself

1 Correct the mistakes in this conversation.

JANE: Where do you stay this week? In a hotel?

RIGGERT: Yes, I staying in a little hotel near the conference centre.

JANE: So, enjoy you the conference?

RIGGERT: No, I not enjoy it. I hate conferences!

2 Read about more individuals and organisations in and around Stockholm. Choose the correct form of the verb to complete the sentences.

1 Nextweb *designs / is designing* websites. Right now we *design / are designing* a website for an important Swedish orchestra.

2 I work for Sadra. It *produces / is producing* paper.

3 I'm an HR manager for SAB. We *launch / are launching* some new Internet banking services at the moment.

4 I have my own consulting company. This week I *run / am running* a team-building course for a client near Stockholm.

5 Hans and I *work / are working* as chemical engineers for Entel AB, a pharmaceutical company. This month we *work / are working* on the design of new sun creams.

3 Complete the dialogue between Helge and Lars, using the present simple or present continuous.

HELGE: Hi, Lars. What (1) .... (you / work on) at the moment?

LARS: I'm so busy! We (2) .... (reorganise) the department right now and it's a lot of work.

HELGE: Really? Where's Anita?

LARS: Anita (3) .... (not / work) this week. She's on holiday. What about you? Are you busy?

HELGE: Very busy. I (4) .... (work) on a new marketing project.

LARS: Really, but you always say you (5) .... (not / like) marketing!

HELGE: Yeah, but actually, this project is quite interesting. We (6) .... (develop) a new sun cream.

LARS: Does the market need another sun cream?

HELGE: Oh, yes. More and more people (7) .... (travel) abroad these days.

LARS: Lucky people. I never (8) .... (go) on holiday – I don't have the time.

Does the market need another sun cream?

Now listen and check. ▶▶|16.2

Sentence stress

1 Look at these three sentences. Which one do you think takes more time to say?

1 One, two, three.

2 I'm working on a special project.

3 Are you staying in a hotel near here?

Now listen and check. ▶▶|16.3

In English, we stress the words in sentences which are important to communicate our ideas. All three sentences above have three main stresses and take about the same time to say even though some are longer than others. Stressed words are spoken with more power and sound than unstressed words.

2 Listen to the following dialogue and underline the stressed words in each sentence. ▶▶|16.4

A: Are you working from home next week?

B: Yes, I'm working from home to the end of the month.

A: Are you busy?

B: Yes, but I'm enjoying the work.

Now practise reading the conversation aloud with a partner.

3 Here are the stressed words from five questions. Make questions using the words.

1 working / hard / this week? *Are you working hard this week?*

2 reading / good / book / moment?

3 enjoying / lesson?

4 What / doing?

5 having / good time?

Now ask your partner the questions. Stress the right words.

It's time to talk

You are away on a training course, staying in a hotel. You want to talk to the other participants in the coffee break. Student A should look at the information on page 105 and Student B at page 107. Ask each other questions and take notes about the following.

| Job |

| Company |

| Hotel |

| Current project |

| Enjoying project? |

Remember

Remember the difference between talking about general and temporary situations.

General situations:
• Riggert works for the Swedish Railroad Authority.
Temporary situations:
• At the moment Riggert is working on a bridge project.

On the agenda

Speaking
Managerial qualities

Communicating at work
Emails 2: Replying to emails

Vocabulary
Communication verbs

Paula Morris is a senior marketing manager for a British publishing company. Read about her work with video-conferencing.

17 Workplace communication

Warm up

Do you use all four of these ways to communicate at work? Which is the best for you? Why?

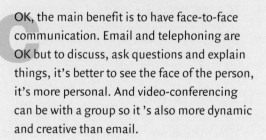

Read on

Communication of the future

1 We interviewed Paula about using video-conferencing. Match our questions with Paula's answers.

1 What are the benefits of video-conferencing?

2 How often do you use video-conferencing?

3 Do you think it has a good future?

4 What problems do you have?

A We meet and talk via the Internet once a month, which is great! In the past we spoke on the phone or sent emails and then travelled to New York for our marketing meetings, usually twice a year. We have much more communication now.

B Well, it's difficult at first. There's a delay with the voice, so you wait after people speak to hear the words. So the main problem is that the process can be a little slow and unnatural sometimes. Also, there are technical problems from time to time. The screen freezes or the system crashes. But sometimes, when someone talks and the voice breaks up, it can be quite funny!

C OK, the main benefit is to have face-to-face communication. Email and telephoning are OK but to discuss, ask questions and explain things, it's better to see the face of the person, it's more personal. And video-conferencing can be with a group so it 's also more dynamic and creative than email.

D Air travel can be expensive and some people don't like flying. So video-conferencing has a very good future. But it's also a little expensive, you need a lot of equipment, and the communication process is not perfect. It's difficult to interrupt, so if some people speak a lot and you are listening and listening to them, it can be very boring. So I'm not sure about the future. I like it but I know some of my colleagues really hate it!

2 Answer these questions about Paula and video-conferencing.

1 Why did Paula travel to New York twice a year?
2 Why is it sometimes difficult to understand people in a video-conference?
3 Why is a video-conference meeting better than a telephone meeting?
4 Why is video-conferencing expensive?

What do you think?   Do you work with video-conferencing?
Would you like to? Why? Why not?

The words you need ... to talk about communication

1 Complete the sentences from Paula's last presentation via video-conference with one of the words in the box.

Beginning the presentation

Today, I would like to (1) .... about our new marketing plan.
If you don't understand anything, I am happy to (2) .... it again.
If you would like to (3) .... a question, please (4) .... me.

Ending the presentation

Thank you for (5) ....
If you would like more information, please (6) .... me by email. Or you can (7) .... me on 0044 1904 566568.

> contact
> explain
> call
> ask
> talk
> listening
> interrupt

Test your partner   Read the sentences from the presentation *without* the communication verbs and see if your partner can repeat the sentence *with* the verb.

2 Read these communication ideas for the perfect manager. Choose the correct verb to complete the sentences.

The perfect manager ...

1 takes his/her team out for a meal every month to *discuss / speak* problems.
2 *tells / speaks* to every team member individually once a day.
3 *listens to / listens* staff ideas and opinions very carefully.
4 *writes / replies to* emails on the same day.
5 *reads / writes* the internal newsletter on the intranet every day.
6 *telephones to / calls* customers every week to see if they have any problems.
7 *asks to / asks* his/her staff for ideas.
8 never *interrupts / explains* people in a meeting.

Perfect managers take their teams
out for a meal every month.

It's time to talk

Which ideas above do you like? Which ideas don't you like? With a partner, make a list of five important qualities for a manager, beginning with the most important. You can use the ideas above and add ideas of your own. Then compare with the class and explain your list.

Top five qualities for a manager:

1 _____

2 _____

3 _____

4 _____

5 _____

Communicating at work

Emails 2: Replying to emails

1 Here is a reply to an email. Complete it with the sentences in the box.

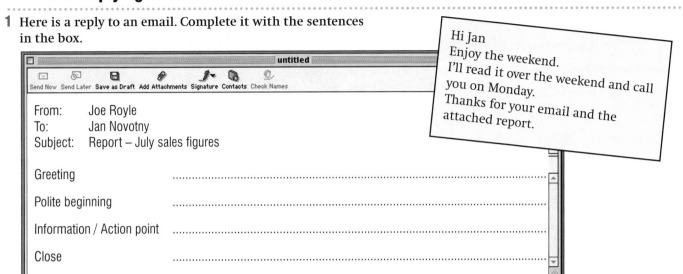

From: Joe Royle
To: Jan Novotny
Subject: Report – July sales figures

Greeting   ....

Polite beginning ....

Information / Action point ....

Close   ....

Hi Jan
Enjoy the weekend.
I'll read it over the weekend and call you on Monday.
Thanks for your email and the attached report.

2 Match the four polite beginnings (1–4) to the correct information / action point (a–d).

1 Nice to hear from you and great news that you're coming!
2 Thanks for your general enquiry about our products and prices.
3 Thanks for the report.
4 Thank you for your email.

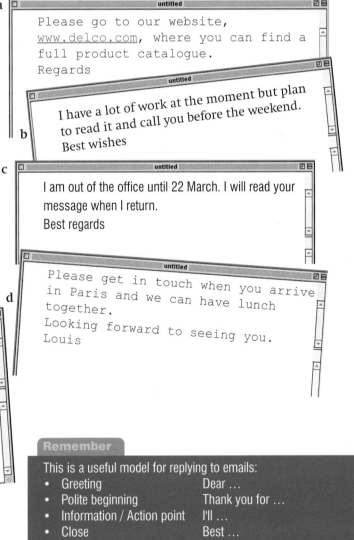

a

Please go to our website, www.delco.com, where you can find a full product catalogue.
Regards

b

I have a lot of work at the moment but plan to read it and call you before the weekend.
Best wishes

c

I am out of the office until 22 March. I will read your message when I return.
Best regards

d

Please get in touch when you arrive in Paris and we can have lunch together.
Looking forward to seeing you.
Louis

3 Reply to the two emails below.

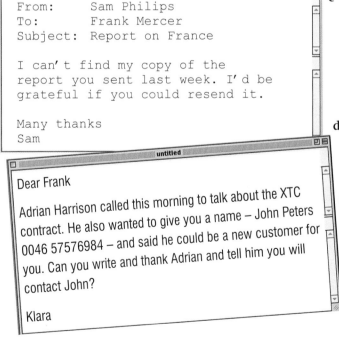

From: Sam Philips
To: Frank Mercer
Subject: Report on France

I can't find my copy of the report you sent last week. I'd be grateful if you could resend it.

Many thanks
Sam

Dear Frank

Adrian Harrison called this morning to talk about the XTC contract. He also wanted to give you a name – John Peters 0046 57576984 – and said he could be a new customer for you. Can you write and thank Adrian and tell him you will contact John?

Klara

Remember

This is a useful model for replying to emails:
* Greeting   Dear …
* Polite beginning   Thank you for …
* Information / Action point   I'll …
* Close   Best …

On the agenda

Speaking
Eating out

Social phrases
At the restaurant

Vocabulary
Food and drink

18 Slow food

How often do you eat out? Which is your favourite restaurant?

Restaurant talk

1 Complete the dialogues with phrases (a–j) below.

At the restaurant

A: Good evening. (1) .... My name's Brillakis.
B: Yes, the table by the window. Can I take your coats?
A: Thank you.
C: Thanks.
B: So, the menu and (2) .... Would you like a drink before you order?

Before the meal

B: (3) .... ?
C: Yes. We'll both have the pâté (4) .... , please. What's John Dory?
B: John Dory is a kind of white sea fish.
C: Then I'll have the John Dory.
A: The salmon, please.
B: Right. And to drink?
A: We'll have (5) ....

During the meal

B: (6) .... ?
C: Yes, thanks. Oh, can I have some more bread, please?
B: Sure. And would you like some more wine?
A: No, thanks. Actually, could we have (7) .... ?

After the meal

B: So, did you enjoy your meal?
C: Yes, thank you. (8) ....
B: Good. And would you like anything else? (9) .... ?
C: No, thank you. (10) .... , please?
B: Of course.

a It was very nice
b the wine list
c Could we have the bill
d Are you ready to order
e a bottle of the house white
f as a starter

g More coffee
h Is everything all right
i I have a reservation
j a bottle of sparkling mineral water

Have a go

Cover the dialogues above and make your own, starting with the words below.

At the restaurant	During the meal
Good evening ...	Is everything ... ?
Before the meal	After the meal
Are you ready ... ?	So, did you enjoy ... ?

2 Now listen and check. ▶▶18.1

3 Practise reading the dialogues with a partner.

Listen to this

A great place to eat

1 What do you know about the Slow Food movement? Listen and number the facts in the order in which Wendy Fogarty talks about them. ▶▶|18.2

The Slow Food movement ...

☐ prefers food which is local and simple.

☐ wants to see good service in restaurants.

☐ was established in Italy in 1986.

☐ is against intensive farming.

☐ became international in 1989.

2 Listen again and answer the questions. ▶▶|18.2

1 Why did the movement begin in Italy?

2 Why does Wendy dislike intensive farming?

3 Where does Fergus Henderson get his products from?

4 Complete Wendy's words: 'Slow means good – good .... and good ....'

Wendy Fogarty is a member of the Slow Food movement, which promotes high quality restaurants and food.

| What do you think? | Do you think all fast food is bad? Why? Why not?

The words you need ... for eating and drinking

1 Complete the sentences with the correct word from the box.

1 Chow Mein is a popular Chinese ....

2 You put your food on a .... and eat from it.

3 The first course in a three-course meal is the ....

4 After the main course, you can also eat a ....

5 Some people prefer French .... to Chinese. Some prefer Italian.

Which dishes are famous in your country?

cuisine
dessert
plate
starter
dish

2 Look at the different types of food and drink. Match the correct heading to each group of words.

1 pork, beef, lamb ....
2 crab, lobster, prawn ....
3 cod, salmon, John Dory ....
4 carrot, potato, pea ....
5 orange, pineapple, cherry ....
6 wine, beer, orange juice ....

> vegetables
> meat
> drinks
> seafood
> fish
> fruit

How many more words can you add to each group? Ask your partner to tell you about his/her favourite food.

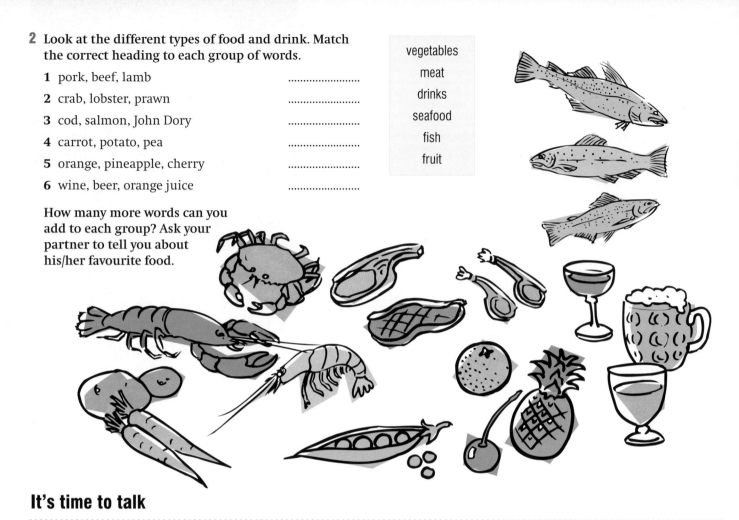

It's time to talk

Work with a partner. You are in a restaurant together. The last person to finish the game pays the bill. You each need a counter. Toss a coin to move. Heads, move two squares. Tails, move one square. On each square, follow the instructions. If you use incorrect language, you must go back one square.

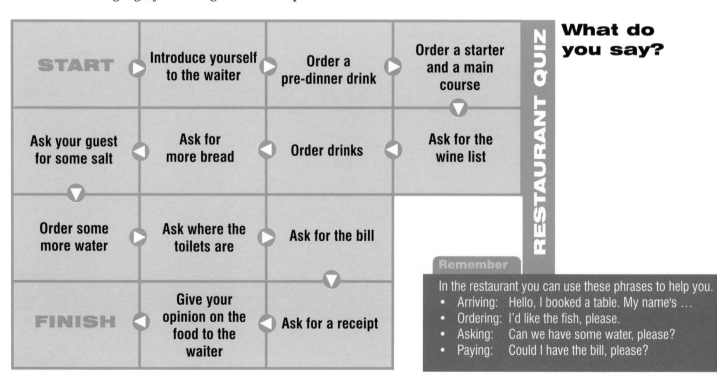

RESTAURANT QUIZ

What do you say?

START ▷	Introduce yourself to the waiter ▷	Order a pre-dinner drink ▷	Order a starter and a main course ▽
Ask your guest for some salt ◁	Ask for more bread ◁	Order drinks ◁	Ask for the wine list
Order some more water ▷	Ask where the toilets are ▷	Ask for the bill ▽	
FINISH ◁	Give your opinion on the food to the waiter ◁	Ask for a receipt	

Remember

In the restaurant you can use these phrases to help you.
- Arriving: Hello, I booked a table. My name's …
- Ordering: I'd like the fish, please.
- Asking: Can we have some water, please?
- Paying: Could I have the bill, please?

On the agenda

Speaking
Organising a visit to
another country

Grammar
Should and *have to*

Pronunciation
Word stress

John Duncan is an English teacher and writer who has lived in Hong Kong.

19 Living in Hong Kong

Warm up

What do you know about Hong Kong?

Listen to this

Chinese culture

1 We interviewed John Duncan about life in Hong Kong. Listen to him talking. Are these sentences true or false? ▶▶|**19.1**

1 You can use first names immediately with all people in Hong Kong.   T ☐ F ☐

2 It's very important to be on time for business meetings.   T ☐ F ☐

3 You can ask people about their salary in general conversation.   T ☐ F ☐

4 Most people dress informally at work.   T ☐ F ☐

2 Listen again and answer these questions. ▶▶|**19.1**

1 What are the 'two Hong Kongs' John talks about?
2 Why is it difficult for big families to live together?
3 How much should you tip in a restaurant?
4 Why do tourists on underground trains sometimes get angry?

What do you think?   What are the big differences between Hong Kong and where you live?

Check your grammar

Should and *have to*

We can use *should* when we want to recommend something. We can use *have to* when we talk about rules that somebody else has made. Look at the examples below (1–4) and match them with the explanations (a–d).

Explanation

1 You should dress well in Hong Kong.   ....

2 You shouldn't forget the tip.   ....

3 You have to use the surname.   ....

4 You don't have to wear designer labels.   ....

a It's not necessary.

b I think it's a good idea.

c It's the rule.

d I think it's a bad idea.

Grammar reference page 117 ▶

Do it yourself

1 Correct the mistakes in these sentences.

1 You haven't to use surnames with the younger generation in Hong Kong.
2 You shouldn't to disagree with your boss in a meeting.
3 Have I dress formally for the meeting?
4 He doesn't have to smoke in here. People are trying to eat.

Should I call him Eddy or Mr Cheung?

2 James Bell is travelling to Sri Lanka. Complete the emails to and from Anne-Marie, his personal assistant, with either *should*, *shouldn't*, *have to* or *don't have to*.

1

□	untitled	回回

Hi Anne-Marie
I (1) .... have a visa to work in Sri Lanka. Please phone the embassy to get the necessary forms.
James

2

Hi James
Got your visa today and some good news. The embassy confirmed that you (2) .... have a vaccination for yellow fever so I cancelled your appointment with the doctor. And I was right about the tap water. The embassy recommended that you (3) .... drink bottled water because the tap water isn't safe.
Anne-Marie

3

□	untitled	回回

Dear Anne-Marie
James Bell's ticket is in the internal mail. Please note that James (4) .... check in at Terminal 1. I checked about hand luggage as you asked and the airline told me that James (5) .... take more than one piece.

---

3 James is now working in Sri Lanka. He is talking to his new colleague. Match her answers to his questions.

Questions

1 Do you have to start work at the same time every day?
2 Do you have to work 40 hours every week?
3 Do you have to wear a tie at work?
4 Should I buy my boss a present? It's her birthday tomorrow.
5 Should I inform Peter about the computer problem?
6 Should I send him an email to confirm the meeting?

Answers

a Yes, you should, but just something simple and not too expensive.
b No. You can choose any time between 7.30 and 9.30.
c Yes, I think you should. He wants to know about any IT questions.
d You don't have to unless you are meeting a customer.
e No, you don't have to. I've already told him the time and place.
f Yes, you have to work the hours in your contract.

Now listen and check. ▶▶**19.2**

Do you have to wear a tie at work?

Word stress

1 When we pronounce words with more than one syllable, we stress one syllable more than the other(s). Listen to the example. ▶▶|19.3

China	Chinese

2 Listen to the extracts from John Duncan's interview and mark the main stress in the words in *italics*. ▶▶|19.4

1 Yeah, it was a *fantastic* time …

2 It's a very *dynamic* place …

3 With a *traditional* person …

4 People are very open about *money* …

5 Hong Kong is a very *fashionable* place …

6 I think family is very *important* …

7 … *modern* houses and flats …

8 … ten or 15 *per cent* …

Pronunciation quiz Write down ten words with two or more syllables you have learnt in earlier units. Use a dictionary to check the stress in each word. Then test your partner by asking him/her to pronounce the words. Does he/she pronounce them correctly?

It's time to talk

Work with a partner. Student A should look at page 105, and Student B at page 108.

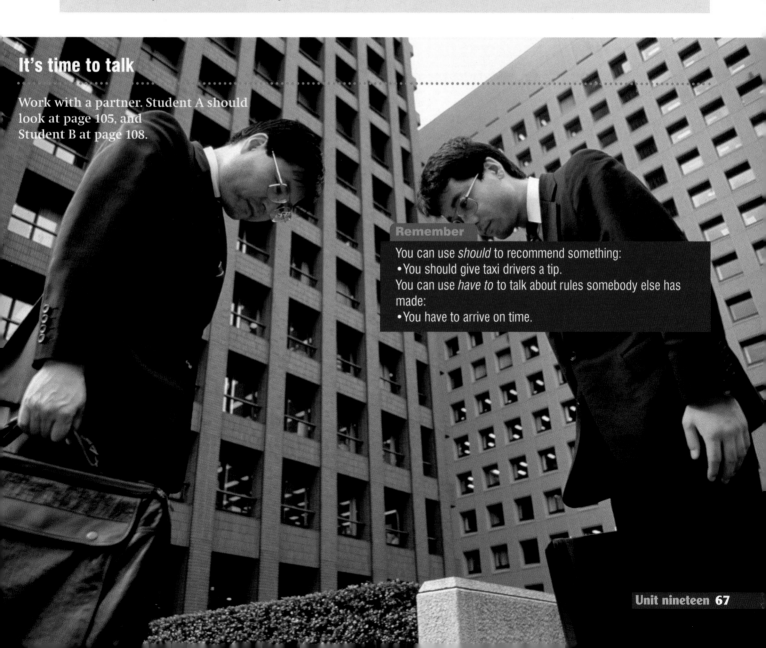

Remember

You can use *should* to recommend something:
• You should give taxi drivers a tip.
You can use *have to* to talk about rules somebody else has made:
• You have to arrive on time.

On the agenda

Speaking
People and their computers

Communicating at work
Telephoning 3: Arranging meetings

Vocabulary
Computers and the Internet

Meet Mike Parker and his family from Boston.

20 Online

Warm up

Do you use a computer?
What do you use it for?
What do your friends and family use it for?
Do you like working with computers?

Read on

Computer heaven or hell?

1 We interviewed Mike Parker about the role computers play in his family's life. Match the headings with his answers.

1 Creating websites
2 Buying online
3 Solving problems
4 Learning Spanish

A
I give technical help to people with computer problems in the company. I get a lot of angry emails every day from people with problems: people can't log on, people can't open their emails or attached files, people say their computer is too slow, some people can't remember their password. I usually get over 50 emails a day because I work in a big company. It's absolutely crazy.

B
With the arrival of the Internet, the biggest change is that Lauren now does most of our shopping online. It's great because it's really easy. She just logs on to our online supermarket or clothes store and buys what we need. Most shops send the products the next day. It's a little more expensive but we both really hate shopping in real shops and so are happy to pay a little more.

C
Martha is 15. She has a PC in her room and she uses the Internet all the time. Of course, she gets information for her schoolwork but she also spends a lot of time in chat rooms talking to friends all over the world. It's good for her Spanish because she can practise with friends in Mexico and Argentina. For her, the Internet is fantastic.

D
George, my son, is 19. He's studying hard at the moment and wants to be a website designer. In fact he's already helped design sites for a couple of local businesses. His girlfriend hates computers and thinks we all spend too much time in front of the PC and I agree. Sometimes he doesn't move for more than 12 hours. I think out of all of us his life is most dominated by the computer.

2 Answer these questions about Mike Parker and computers.

1 How many emails does Mike get every day?
2 Why do Mike and Lauren use the Internet for shopping?
3 What does Martha use the Internet for?
4 How long does George sometimes spend on the computer?

What do you think? 'We all spend too much time in front of the PC.'
Do you agree?

The words you need ... to talk about computers and the Internet

1 Use the verbs in the box to complete these emails sent to Mike by computer users.
Use the correct form of the verb.

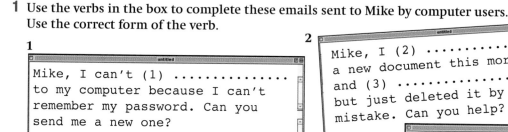

1
Mike, I can't (1) ....
to my computer because I can't
remember my password. Can you
send me a new one?

2
Mike, I (2) ....
a new document this morning
and (3) ....it
but just deleted it by
mistake. Can you help?

3
Mike, I can't open and
(4) .... the
attached file you sent me. Can
you (5) .... it,
please?

resend
save
create
log on
print

Now match a reply to each of the emails.

a Go to 'Deleted items' and you will find your new file.
b Attached file is unzipped WORD document so will open OK.
c Enter MEMORY as your new username and password.

What computer problems do you have at work?

2 Complete the Internet information in Mike's company with words from the box.

surf   intranet   virus
online   chat   connect

Do

1 .... to the company network if you want to work from home.
2 search for business information .... if you need to.
3 use the .... to learn about company news.

Don't

4 .... on websites in work time for private use.
5 download files which may have a ....
6 connect to Internet .... rooms when at work.

Does your organisation have any rules about using the Internet?

It's time to talk

Read what people say about using the computer and Internet at work and at home.

Work
I never print my emails. It uses too much paper.

I always create a password with my wife's name so I can't forget!

I delete all old emails at the end of each day.

I read the company news on the intranet every day.

I work from home two days a week by connecting to my office computer.

Home
I practise my English in chat rooms on the Internet.

I download free music from the Internet.

I book all my holiday travel on the Internet.

I surf for English websites which have free grammar and vocabulary exercises.

Work with a partner. Does he/she do the same as the people above? Why? Why not?

Communicating at work

Telephoning 3: Arranging meetings

1 Listen to three people arranging three meetings with Jim, an operations controller. Match the people with the correct day and time. ▶▶|20.1

Person	Meeting day	Meeting time
1 Philippe	Monday	10.00
2 Frank	Tuesday	11.00
3 Petra	Wednesday	12.00
	Thursday	13.00
	Friday	14.00

2 Listen again and tick the sentences you hear. ▶▶|20.1

Is it possible to have a meeting? ▢

Is Friday morning convenient? ▢

See you next week. ▢

I'm sorry, I can't. ▢

When are you free? ▢

Sorry, I can't make Friday morning. ▢

I'm calling to fix a meeting. ▢

See you on Tuesday at 10. ▢

3 Work with a partner. Make two phone calls to arrange meetings using the notes in your diary. One of you is A and the other is B. Use the diagram to help you. Student A should look at the diary for Monday 23rd and phone Student B.

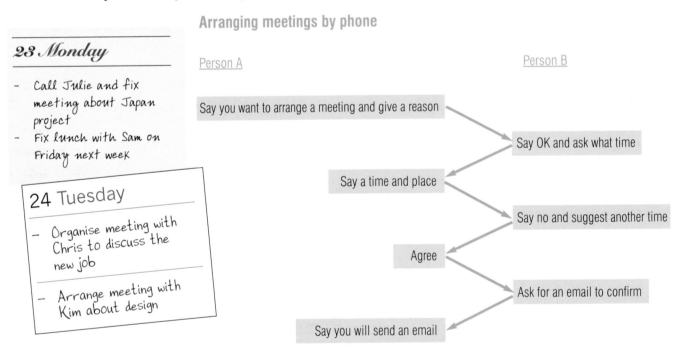

23 Monday

- Call Julie and fix meeting about Japan project
- Fix lunch with Sam on Friday next week

24 Tuesday

- Organise meeting with Chris to discuss the new job
- Arrange meeting with Kim about design

Arranging meetings by phone

Person A — Say you want to arrange a meeting and give a reason

Person B — Say OK and ask what time

Say a time and place

Say no and suggest another time

Agree

Ask for an email to confirm

Say you will send an email

Now Student B should look at the diary for Tuesday 24th and phone Student A.

Remember

When arranging meetings by phone:
- Start politely: Is it possible to have a meeting?
- Be open: When is it convenient?
- Confirm: So, Tuesday at 10.
- Finish positively: See you on Tuesday.

On the agenda

Speaking
Hotels

Social phrases
Staying in a hotel

Vocabulary
Hotels and hotel service

Warm up

Which three things are most important to you when you stay in a hotel?

21 Beirut Intercontinental

Enjoy your stay

1 Complete the dialogues with the phrases (a–j) below.

Checking in

A: Hello, my name's Sanchez, (1) ....
B: Good evening. Yes, Mr Sanchez, (2) .... , for two nights. Could you complete this form, please?
A: Of course.
B: Thank you. So, it's room 414, on the fourth floor. Do you need any help with your bags?
A: No, thanks. (3) ....

A morning call

A: Hello, can I have (4) .... , please? At 7 o'clock?
B: Certainly, sir.
A: So (5) .... at 6.30. Can you do that?
B: That's fine. So, morning call at 6.30, breakfast at 7 o'clock.

A problem

A: Good morning. There's a problem with the shower. (6) .... Can you send someone to look at it?
B: Of course, I'll send someone immediately. (7) .... ?
A: 414.
B: Fine. Someone will be with you in a moment.

Leaving

A: Morning, (8) .... , please? Room 414.
B: Right, Mr Sanchez. (9) .... last night?
A: No, nothing.
B: OK, (10) .... Sign here, please. Have a good trip home.

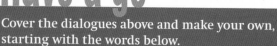

a here's your bill
b I'd like a wake-up call
c Anything from the minibar
d can I check out
e I can manage
f breakfast in my room
g I have a reservation
h a single room
i There's no hot water
j What's your room number

Have a go

Cover the dialogues above and make your own, starting with the words below.

Checking in
Hello, my name's ...

A problem
Good morning. There's a problem ...

A morning call
Hello, can I have ...

Leaving
Morning, can I ...

2 Now listen and check. ▶▶ 21.1

3 Practise reading the dialogues with a partner.

Listen to this

It's a great place to stay

1 We interviewed Bob Hands about his favourite hotel. Listen and decide which picture he describes. ▶▶|21.2

2 Now listen again. Are these sentences true or false? ▶▶|21.2

  1 It is a five-star hotel.   T ☐ F ☐

  2 It has an excellent Spanish restaurant.   T ☐ F ☐

  3 Hotel staff meet you at the airport.   T ☐ F ☐

  4 Sidney's is a famous restaurant near the hotel.   T ☐ F ☐

What do you think? Do you have any favourite hotels? What are they called? Why do you like them?

Bob Hands spends more than 200 nights a year in hotels, so he knows which ones he likes.

The words you need ... for staying in hotels

connect	key	change
towels	cancel	double room
recommend	corridor	

1 Complete the sentences with the correct word from the box.

  1 I'm sorry but I can't find my room .... Could I have another?

  2 I'm afraid I have to .... my reservation.

  3 Can you .... a restaurant near here?

  4 How much is a .... for two nights, please?

  5 There are no clean .... in the room. Could you send some up?

  6 Can I .... my room, please? This one is too noisy.

  7 Excuse me, is the swimming pool down this .... ?

  8 Can you .... me to Janet Ward in room 320, please?

2 Match up the problems with the correct picture.

<u>Problem</u>

1 It's empty.
2 It doesn't open.
3 It's too dark to read.
4 The picture is terrible.
5 It's very dirty.

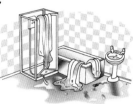

We can use *I'll* + verb when we promise to do something.

Example: GUEST: It's the minibar. It's empty.

RECEPTIONIST: I'll send someone to your room immediately.

Look again at problems 2–5 above. You are the receptionist in a hotel.
Get your partner to read out the problems; you promise to help. Then change roles.

It's time to talk

The hotel game

This is a game for two to four players. Toss a coin to move. Heads move two squares. Tails move one square. When you land on a square, say what the instruction on the square tells you to say. If the other players are happy that the English is correct, you stay on the square. If not, move back. If you disagree with your colleagues, your teacher will rule. The winner is the first guest to check out.

Ring the hotel **Ask the price of a single room**	**Ring the hotel** **Book a room**	**Ring the hotel** **You have a reservation for next Tuesday; change it**	**Ring the hotel** **You want to speak to Mrs Johnson in room 274**
Go to reception **You want to change your room; say why**	**Return to reception** **Tell them you've lost your key**	**Phone reception** **Ask if you can send an email**	**Arrive at the hotel** **Check in**
Go to reception **Ask where the swimming pool is located in the hotel**	**Phone reception** **Ask for a morning call**	**Go to reception** **The hotel restaurant is busy; ask about restaurants near the hotel**	**Phone reception** **The people in the next room are very noisy and you can't sleep**
		Go to reception **CHECK OUT**	**Go to reception** **You need a taxi to the airport tomorrow morning**

Remember

Remember to learn the phrases in the unit for when you stay in a hotel.
- Arriving: I have a reservation.
- Asking for information: What time is breakfast?
- Complaining: My shower doesn't work.
- Leaving: I'd like to check out, please.

On the agenda

Speaking
Numbers and quantity

Grammar
Many, much, a few, a little

Pronunciation
Saying numbers and prices

Isabelle Segura is a PA in Neuilly, just outside Paris. She talks about her working week.

22 Working for Rolls Royce

Warm up

How many hours per week do you work?
Do you think you work too much?

Listen to this

Work is like a second home

1 Listen to Isabelle Segura talking about her job in Rolls Royce International. Which of the details are correct? ▶▶|22.1

2 Listen again and answer the following questions. ▶▶|22.1

   1 What's the first thing Isabelle does when she gets to work?
   2 How much time does Isabelle spend reading and writing her emails?
   3 What benefits does Isabelle get in her job?
   4 Why does she like her job?

Number of employees	4	40	400	
Meetings per week	2–3	4–5	more than 5	
Working hours per week	30	35	40	
Holiday weeks per year	3	5	6	

What do you think?   Isabelle says: 'People spend too much time in meetings.' Is it the same in your organisation?

Check your grammar

Many, much, a few, a little

We can use *many, much, a few* and *a little* to talk about quantity. Look at the examples below.

I don't have many meetings today.

I don't have much time.

I need a little information.

I have a few jobs for you to do.

How much work have you got to do?

How many business trips does he make each year?

Can I have a little more time?

Do you have a few more minutes?

Now complete these rules with *many, much, a few* or *a little*.

We use *many* and (1) .... with countable nouns.

We use (2) .... and *a little* with uncountable nouns.

We use (3) .... and *much*, mainly in questions and negatives.

We use *a few* and (4) .... mainly in positives and questions.

Note
Remember that we can use *a lot of* in positives, negatives and questions with countable plural nouns and uncountable nouns. See Unit 7.

Grammar reference page 118 ▐▐▶

Do it yourself

1 Correct the mistakes in these sentences.

  1 I don't give much presentations in my job.
  2 Do you want a few milk with your coffee?
  3 How many information do you have about our new product?
  4 I'm sorry but I need a few more time to write this report.

2 Complete the questions with *How many* **or** *How much*.

  1 How .... cars has he got?
  2 How .... information does he have?
  3 How .... people work in production?
  4 How .... new equipment have they bought?
  5 How .... jobs does she have?
  6 How .... meetings do you have this week?
  7 How .... money does he make?
  8 How .... emails have I got?

3 Choose the correct word or phrase to complete the email. Sometimes more than one answer is possible.

many	a little	a few	much	a lot of

From: Arthur Davies, CEO, Davies Software
To: Patricia Delmont, Delmont Travel
Subject: Late delivery

Dear Ms Delmont,

I'm very sorry that your software is late. We had (1) .... problems in production this week. I'm afraid I can't give you (2) .... information at the moment. We will need (3)................ time before we can begin production again, but only (4) .... days.

I hope this will not give you too (5) .... problems.

Best regards,
Arthur Davies

A few production problems

4 Write some sentences about your job.

  Example: I go to too many meetings each week.

  1 .... a lot of ....
  2 .... many ....
  3 .... much ....
  4 .... a few ....
  5 .... a little ....

Saying numbers and prices

1 In pairs, write down how to say these numbers and prices. Some answers are given for you.

Numbers		Prices	
25	twenty-five	50p	....
100	....	£4.99	....
101	....	£250	two hundred and fifty pounds
1,000	....	€150,000	....
2,001	....	£150m	....
10,550	....	$0.99	....
500,000	five hundred thousand	$4.95	....
1,000,000	....	$2,500	two thousand five hundred dollars
1,000,000,000	....	$2.5m	....

2 Listen and check your answers. ▶▶|22.2

Test your partner Cover your partner's answers. Then point at some of the numbers and prices above and ask your partner to say them.

" Can you say this? "

" Yes. That's two thousand five hundred dollars. "

3 Write down five numbers (big and small) and five prices (euros, pounds and dollars). Then dictate the numbers to your partner.

Numbers	Prices
....	....
....	....
....	....
....	....
....	....

It's time to talk

You are going to role-play a conversation with your partner. Student A should look at page 105 and Student B at page 108.

Remember

When talking about numbers and quantity, remember to:
Use *How many* with countable nouns:
• How many sales people are going to the exhibition?
Use *How much* with uncountable nouns:
• How much exhibition space do we have?

On the agenda

Speaking
Solving a business problem

Communicating at work
Helping visitors

Vocabulary
Money and business finance

Jackie Black started a delicatessen, the Tower Street Pantry, four years ago, in York, England.

23 Start up

Warm up

Is it easy to start a business in your country?
Would you like to have your own business?
Why? Why not?
What kind of business would you start?

Read on

Managing a small business

1 We interviewed Jackie Black about the business she and her husband started. Match the questions with her answers.

1 And what are your plans for the future?
2 Do you recommend starting a business?
3 Did you need to borrow from the bank?
4 What kind of business is it?
5 What are your major costs?

A Well, we started the Tower Street Pantry four years ago as a sandwich bar. We were bored with the fact that so much food is pre-packed, in plastic triangles, or from designer cafés, and we wanted to do something fresh, freshly made. That's what people like.

B No, nothing. At the beginning, of course, we went to the bank with a business plan and they offered to lend us money. Then a member of our family also offered us the money – interest free – so we borrowed it from them. And we earned enough to pay it back in the first year, which was great.

C It was staff, but now I think it's fresh fruit and vegetables. It sounds crazy but when the bad weather comes you have to pay a lot for fresh vegetables, and we only use fresh vegetables, so it's expensive.

D Well, business is getting stronger and stronger. Turnover is increasing all the time. And last year profits doubled. But we plan to do lunches for companies soon, that kind of thing. It's very interesting because the margin is a lot higher. And we like making money!

E Oh, yes. I love having a business because what we do is very people-orientated, it's a service really, more than just a shop. People need us. But you have problems, of course. The biggest is staff! You can't get good staff. This means sometimes we have to do everything. So, believe me, managing a business can be really, really hard work.

2 Read the interview again and answer the questions.

   1 When did Jackie and her husband start the Tower Street Pantry?

   2 Where did Jackie and her husband get the finance to start the business?

   3 What is the biggest cost for Jackie's business now?

   4 How much did profits increase last year?

   5 Why does Jackie want to expand into company lunches?

What do you think? Would you like to run a small business like Jackie's? Why? Why not?

Jackie wants to expand into company lunches.

The words you need ... to talk about money and business finance

1 Complete the article with the correct word from the box.

Use some of the finance words to make sentences about your organisation. For example: 'Last year the turnover of my organisation was £30 million.'

2 Complete Jackie's ideas on financial strategy for next year with the correct money verb.

| pay | borrrow | make | increase | invest |

   1 We're sure we can .... more money next year than this year.

   2 We don't want to .... any money from the bank.

   3 I think we can .... our prices by 5%.

   4 We plan to .... some money in new equipment.

   5 I hope we can .... less tax next year.

Write some sentences using these money verbs.

A success story

Jackie Black's Tower Street Pantry is a success story in York. Every year she has more customers and (1) .... increases. Last year the business made a good (2) .... and Jackie is sure this can continue. Of course, she has to keep control of (3) .... But she also plans to move into corporate lunches where the (4) .... is better. This week is an important week for Jackie as she plans her (5) .... We wish her good luck and every success for next year.

| profit |
| budget |
| turnover |
| margin |
| costs |

It's time to talk

Your organisation is in big trouble. Turnover is down €1m. Work in groups and hold a meeting to decide which of these ideas you should follow to improve the situation.

Now tell the other members of the class what your group decided.

> I think that we should pay all staff 10% less. What do you think?

> I don't agree. I think we should invest less in training. Salary is important for motivation.

Decrease the advertising budget by €550,000

Increase prices by 2%; this will increase turnover by €800,000

Borrow €500,000 from the bank at 6% interest for future investment

Pay all staff 10% less salary for one year; this will save €560,000

Invest €500,000 less in training.

Fly economy class for business travel and reduce costs by €100,000

Communicating at work

Helping visitors

1 What do you do if a visitor to your organisation asks for help? Listen to four dialogues and match each one with a cartoon. ▶▶|23.1

Dialogue	Cartoon
1	
2	
3	
4	

2 Listen again. Which of these sentences do you hear? ▶▶|23.1

<u>Giving help</u>

Do you need any help? ☐

Follow me. ☐

Can I help? ☐

Do you want to borrow some money? ☐

Would you like to use a computer here? ☐

I'm sure I can find one for you. ☐

I can show you on the map, if you want. ☐

3 Look at this framework.

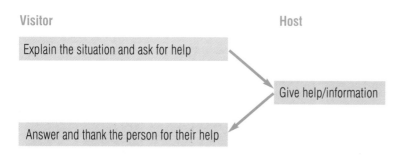

How to take care of a visitor

Visitor — Host

Explain the situation and ask for help

→ Give help/information

Answer and thank the person for their help

Work with a partner. You are helping an important client with a problem. Use the framework to help them with the situations below. Take turns with your partner to play the visitor.

<u>Situations</u>

1 The visitor needs a taxi.
2 The visitor wants help booking a theatre ticket.
3 The visitor wants to send an email to his/her office.
4 The visitor's mobile phone battery is flat.
5 The visitor wants to buy something typical from your region.

> **Remember**
>
> When helping visitors, remember to ask questions and make offers politely:
> - Can I help?
> - Do you need any help?
> - What can I do for you?
> - I can do that for you.

On the agenda

Speaking
Spending

Social phrases
Money talk

Vocabulary
Money and shopping

Warm up

Do you like spending money? What do you like spending money on?

24 I buy money

Money talk

1 Complete the dialogues with phrases (a–j) below.

Asking a colleague for money

A: Clare, I haven't got much cash on me.
B: (1) .... some money?
A: (2) .... ten pounds until tomorrow?
B: No problem.
A: Cheers. That's (3) ....

Getting money out

A: Shall we find a restaurant?
B: Yes, but (4) .... first.
A: OK, I'll wait here.
B: (5) .... ?
A: Yes, there's a bank just across the road, over there.

Changing money

A: Hello, (6) .... into Swiss francs.
B: How much do you want to change?
A: (7) .... ?
B: There's no commission if you change more than 200 euros.
A: OK, then (8) .... , thanks.

Getting change

A: Excuse me, (9) .... ?
B: What do you need?
A: (10) .... for the coffee machine.
B: Just a second, yes, here you are.
A: Thanks very much.

Have a go

a What's the commission	**f** do you have any change
b I need some coins	**g** I need to get some money out
c Is there a cash point nearby	**h** I'll change 300
d Could you lend me	**i** Do you want to borrow
e very nice of you	**j** I'd like to change some euros

Cover the dialogues above and make your own, starting with the words below.

Asking for money	Changing money
I haven't got much ...	Hello, I'd like ...
Getting money out	Getting change
Shall we ... ?	Excuse me, ...

2 Now listen and check. ▶▶24.1

3 Practise reading the dialogues with a partner.

Listen to this

Hey, big spender

1 We interviewed three people about how they like to spend their money. Listen to the conversations and match each person with an illustration below. ▶▶|24.2

Person	Illustration
1	
2	
3	

Anne, Tashi and Sam explain how they spend their money.

2 Listen again and answer the questions. ▶▶|24.2

1 When does Anne go shopping for clothes?
2 Why does Anne save her money?
3 What does Tashi spend his money on?
4 Is Tashi careful with money?
5 What does Sam buy every Saturday morning?
6 How often does Sam buy shoes?

What do you think? Which person do you think manages their money best?

The words you need ... to talk about money

1 Complete the sentences with the correct preposition from the box.

How to be good with money

1 Don't spend money .... things which you don't need.
2 Don't invest .... risky stocks and shares.
3 Don't pay .... everything by credit card.
4 Save money .... shopping in hypermarkets.
5 Shop around .... low prices.
6 Be careful .... your money. Find the lowest prices!

for	on	in
with	by	for

2 When you learn vocabulary, it is helpful to organise your learning around important topics. Complete the boxes with the correct word from the list.

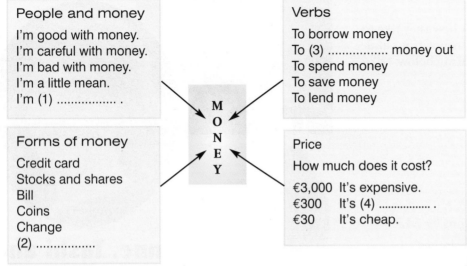

People and money

I'm good with money.
I'm careful with money.
I'm bad with money.
I'm a little mean.
I'm (1) ....

Verbs

To borrow money
To (3) .... money out
To spend money
To save money
To lend money

Forms of money

Credit card
Stocks and shares
Bill
Coins
Change
(2) ....

Price

How much does it cost?

€3,000 It's expensive.
€300   It's (4) ....
€30   It's cheap.

M O N E Y

reasonable

get

notes

generous

Test your partner Close your books. See how many words your partner can remember from each box.

It's time to talk

Are you good with money?

You and your partner win €1,000,000 in the lottery. How do you plan to spend the money? Tick three of the following:

		You	Your partner
1	Pay all your credit card bills immediately		
2	Invest over 30% in a pension		
3	Give 50% to a charity working in Africa		
4	Travel around the world for three months		
5	Spend a lot of money on a new car		
6	Buy a much bigger house		
7	Give or lend money to friends and family		
8	Save over 50% of the money in the bank		
9	Buy expensive clothes and jewellery		

Now ask your partner how he/she plans to spend the money. Note down his/her answers and then turn to page 109 to find out if he/she is good or bad with money!

A: So, what do you plan to spend the money on?

B: Firstly, I plan to buy ...

A: And what else?

B: Then I want to spend some money on ...

Remember

Learn these useful phrases about money:
• Is there a cash point nearby?
• Could you lend me some money?
• Do you have any change?
• I'd like to change some euros.

On the agenda

Speaking
Future plans

Grammar
The present
continuous 2

Pronunciation
Weak stress 2

Meet Anthony Allen. He started SROA – the Selsey Romania Orphans Appeal – and helps children in Romania.

25 Driving to Romania

Warm up

In pairs, ask and answer these questions about the future.

" Are you doing anything special at the weekend? "

" What are you doing tomorrow? "

Listen to this

A job everyone wants to do

1 We interviewed Anthony Allen about his work in Romania. Are these sentences true or false? ▶▶|25.1

1 Anthony started SROA in 1998.   T ☐ F ☐
2 Eight people are travelling to Romania in October.   T ☐ F ☐
3 Anthony is staying in Romania for two weeks in October.   T ☐ F ☐
4 SROA gets most of its money from the government.   T ☐ F ☐

2 Listen again and answer the questions. ▶▶|25.1

1 Why did Anthony start SROA?
2 What was the first objective of SROA in Romania?
3 What is the big project for next year?
4 What salary do people get in SROA?

What do you think? Would you like to do charity work in another country?

Check your grammar

The present continuous 2

In Unit 16, we looked at the present continuous for talking about *temporary* situations with the focus on the present. The present continuous is also useful when you talk about fixed *future* plans, especially for travel and meetings. Complete the questions and answers below.

Question	Positive	Negative
What are you (1) .... next month?	We're driving to Romania.	We're not flying.
How long are you staying?	We (2) .... staying for two weeks.	We're not staying longer than two weeks.

Questions + short answers		
(3) .... you driving to Romania?	Yes, I (4)	No, I'm not.
Are they flying in October?	Yes, they are.	No, they (5) ....

Grammar reference pages 116-17 ▮▮▶

Do it yourself

1 Correct the mistakes in these sentences.

   1 I giving a presentation next week.
   2 Are your boss coming to the meeting?
   3 Do you going to the theatre tonight?
   4 I'm not come to the theatre tonight. I'm tired.

2 Anna is a local project manager in Romania. Anthony rings her to discuss the hospital project for next year. Complete their conversation with the correct form of the present continuous.

ANTHONY: Anna, it's Anthony. I just wanted to discuss the hospital schedule and check you agree with everything.

ANNA: Sure. Go ahead.

ANTHONY: OK, (1) .... (we / not / meet) the architects in October. (2) .... (We / see) them in November instead.

ANNA: Right. So (3) .... (when / you / go) to Bucharest for the meeting with the government officials?

ANTHONY: On 18th December. And just before that, on December 14th, (4) .... (we / run) a seminar to inform everyone in SROA about the project. (5) .... (you / still / come) to England next year?

ANNA: Yes, in January.

ANTHONY: Good. Well, (6) .... (we / have) a tour of my local hospital at the end of January to meet some doctors who are part of the project. I think that's everything.

ANNA: Good. See you soon.

Now listen and check. ▶▶|25.2

3 You received this email from your boss this morning. Write a reply using the notes on page 109. Where possible, use the present continuous.

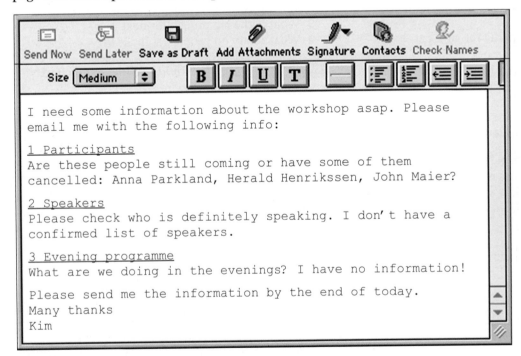

I need some information about the workshop asap. Please email me with the following info:

1 Participants
Are these people still coming or have some of them cancelled: Anna Parkland, Herald Henrikssen, John Maier?

2 Speakers
Please check who is definitely speaking. I don't have a confirmed list of speakers.

3 Evening programme
What are we doing in the evenings? I have no information!

Please send me the information by the end of today.
Many thanks
Kim

With a partner, compare your emails. Can you correct any grammar mistakes?

Weak stress 2

1 Listen to the pronunciation of two questions. Which one sounds more natural? ▶▶|25.3

2 As we saw in Unit 10, unstressed words are often pronounced with the schwa /ə/. Using the schwa correctly is very important for your understanding and pronunciation. Listen and write down the questions you hear. ▶▶|25.4

A: What ....

B: I'm going to Poland.

A: Poland? What ....

B: I'm visiting a friend.

A: How ....

B: Just for a few days.

A: When ....

B: Next Friday.

A: Are ....

B: Yes, I'm going camping.

3 Listen again and underline all the examples of the schwa. ▶▶|25.4

4 With a partner, practise saying the dialogue.

It's time to talk

Student A should look at the information on page 106 and Student B at page 108.

Discussing a trip to Poland.

Remember

When discussing fixed future plans you can use the present continuous:
A: Are you doing anything on Monday morning, Paolo?
B: Yes, I am. I'm meeting Flavia at 9 o'clock.

On the agenda

Speaking
Solving work problems

Vocabulary
Words and expressions
for problem solving

**Communicating at
work**
Telephoning 4: Solving
problems by phone

**Amy Harrison is an
exhibitions manager in
the USA. She had some
problems on her last
trip to Pennsylvania.**

26 Out of order

Warm up

When was the last time you were unhappy about the service you received?
Did you receive good customer service when you complained?

Read on

Problems in Pennsylvania

1 We interviewed Amy about her trip to an
exhibition in Pennsylvania. Match the
headings with her answers.

1 Can we offer you a discount?

2 How was the hotel?

3 Is it turned on?

4 Did you have a good trip?

I planned to fly to Pennsylvania last month for an
exhibition but the flight was cancelled 24 hours
before I travelled. I was really stressed but I
telephoned a travel agent friend who was really
helpful and very quick. He solved the problem by
finding another flight just one hour later.

I had a terrible hotel. The room was cold and the lift
was out of order. The food in the restaurant was
always overcooked and cold. And the staff were rude.
I told the manager about all these problems and she
said she would investigate – but she did nothing. I'll
never stay there again.

I had one really embarrassing moment. During the
exhibition, I bought a new mobile phone. When I
tried it at the hotel it didn't work so I took it back. I
complained but the assistant was very patient. In fact,
he dealt with the problem very quickly – he switched
it on! He was very polite but I felt really stupid.

I ordered some products from a supplier at the
exhibition. I waited for three weeks but nothing
arrived. Finally, I telephoned and explained the
problem to a customer care manager. She said my
order was sent to the wrong address because of a
computer problem. But she was very customer-
friendly: she listened, apologised and then offered
me a 25% discount. Great customer service.

2 Read the text again and answer these questions.

  1 How did Amy find a new flight?
  2 What was wrong with the food in Amy's hotel?
  3 Why did Amy's new mobile phone not work?
  4 What did the customer care manager offer Amy?

What do you think? How customer-friendly is your organisation?
Do you think the customer is always right?

The words you need ... to talk about work problems

1 Look back at the text about Amy. How many verbs can you find that go with the noun *problem*?

2 Here are some sentences about work problems. Are they *time* or *technical* problems?

  Example: The train was one hour late. = Time

  1 My computer crashes every 20 minutes.
  2 It takes me two hours to get to work every day.
  3 We don't have very long to finish the project.
  4 The coffee machine is broken.
  5 I can't open the email attachment.
  6 We can't deliver the order by the end of the month.

  Do you have a time problem at work? What is it?
  Do you have a technical problem at work? What is it?

3 Look at these ways of solving problems with your computer.

  ❝You **should** restart your computer.❞

  ❝You **need to** restart the computer.❞

  ❝**Try** restart**ing** it.❞

Problem solving

Now complete these sentences about different problems.

  1 .... telephone the client immediately and apologise.
  2 .... ask the office to resend the file in a different format.
  3 .... turning it off and on. That sometimes helps!
  4 .... to arrange a meeting to discuss a new schedule.
  5 .... finding a house closer to the office.
  6 .... to upgrade it with more memory.

It's time to talk

You are going to solve your partner's problems. Student A should look at page 106 and Student B at page 109.

Communicating at work

Telephoning 4: Solving problems by phone

1 Complete the three phone conversations with words or phrases from each group.

Explain problem	Ask for help	Offer help	Checking
I didn't get	Could you contact	I'll do	Do you want me to call back after I speak to him?
I can't remember	Could you get someone	I'll call	Is that OK?
I'm having a problem	Could you send	I'll ask	Call me back in 30 minutes if you still haven't got it.

Call 1

MARIA: Hi, Annie. It's Maria. I'm sorry but (1) .... with my computer.

ANNIE: What sort of problem?

MARIA: It keeps crashing for no reason. (2) .... to check it?

ANNIE: Don't worry. (3) .... an engineer to check. (4) ....

MARIA: Wonderful. Thank you. Bye.

Call 2

JULIE: Hello, Annie. It's Julie from Excom. I'm sorry but (5) .... the minutes from our last meeting.

ANNIE: Really? I sent them last week in an attachment.

JULIE: Well, I don't think they arrived. (6) .... them again?

ANNIE: Sure. I'm really sorry about that. (7) .... it now. (8) ....

JULIE: That's great.

Call 3

PETER: Hi, Annie. It's Peter. (9) .... the time of our meeting next week.

ANNIE: Tuesday at 10 o'clock.

PETER: That's fine. (10) .... Jan? I forgot to tell him about it.

ANNIE: Of course. (11) .... him straightaway. (12) ....

PETER: No, only call back if you don't reach him.

2 Listen to check your answers. ▶▶|26.1

3 Think of two typical work problems. Then telephone your partner and ask for help.

Student A   Student B

Explain the problem and ask for help	→	Offer help and check
Thank and say goodbye	→	Say goodbye

> **Remember**
>
> If you have a problem, remember to:
> - explain the problem clearly
> - ask for help politely.
>
> If someone calls you with a problem:
> - show understanding
> - offer help quickly and politely.

On the agenda

Speaking
Decision making

Social phrases
Inviting

Vocabulary
Health

Warm up

When was the last time you invited someone to dinner? Who did you invite? Where did you go?

27 Teaching T'ai Chi

Inviting

1 Complete the dialogues with phrases (a–j) below.

Inviting someone

SUE: Vasili, (1) .... lunch tomorrow after our meeting.

VASILI: Oh, thank you very much.

SUE: There's a Mexican restaurant nearby. (2) .... ?

VASILI: (3) ....

SUE: Good. I'll reserve a table.

Saying 'maybe' to an invitation

SUE: We're having a little party at the weekend. (4) .... ?

BERNDT: That sounds nice. Thank you. (5) ....

SUE: Fine. Can you let me know before Friday?

BERNDT: I'll let you know before then.

Saying 'no' to an invitation

SUE: Michel, I want to try the new vegetarian café across the road. (6) .... ?

MICHEL: (7) .... I have some visitors from the US. (8) ....

SUE: That's OK. Another time.

MICHEL: Definitely.

Cancelling an invitation

Vasili: I'm really sorry Sue, but (9) .... lunch tomorrow. Something's come up.

Sue: No problem.

Vasili: Can we fix another time?

Sue: Let's do something next week.

Vasili: (10) ....

a I have to cancel

b That sounds good

c Can you and Jitka come

d Is that OK for you

e I'd like to invite you to

f Are you free for lunch on Friday

g I'm afraid I can't

h But thanks for the invitation

i Yes, sorry about that

j But I'll have to check with Jitka

Have a go

Cover the dialogues above and make your own, starting with the words below.

Inviting someone	Saying 'no' to an invitation
I'd like to ...	I want to try ...
Saying 'maybe' to an invitation	Cancelling an invitation
We're having a ...	I'm really sorry ...

2 Now listen and check. ▶▶27.1

3 Practise reading the dialogues with a partner.

Listen to this

T'ai Chi can improve your life

1 Listen to Mike Tabrett talking about T'ai Chi. Are these sentences true or false? ▶▶|27.2

1 T'ai Chi is different from Kung Fu.   T ☐   F ☐

2 Mike's oldest student is 65 years old.   T ☐   F ☐

3 Mike is a vegetarian.   T ☐   F ☐

4 Mike never does T'ai Chi classes with companies.   T ☐   F ☐

2 Listen again and answer the questions. ▶▶|27.2

1 There are four elements to T'ai Chi. Breathing, body position and soft movements are the first three. What is the fourth element?

2 What is the main benefit of T'ai Chi?

3 Mike thinks T'ai Chi is better than sport? Why?

4 What should we do every day for two minutes?

| What do you think? | Mike says: 'You should do T'ai Chi because I think it can improve your life!' Would you like to try T'ai Chi?

Meet Mike Tabrett who teaches T'ai Chi. He talks to us about T'ai Chi and how to stay healthy.

The words you need ... to talk about health

1 Match the health advice with the correct illustration.

1 You should drink two litres of water every day. ☐

2 You shouldn't eat too much junk food. ☐

3 You should exercise regularly. ☐

4 You should think carefully about what food you buy. ☐

5 You shouldn't smoke. ☐

6 You shouldn't go to bed too late. ☐

With a partner, think of two or more sentences giving advice about health. Then tell the class.

2 Complete these sentences with a word from the box.

1 I want to .... weight but at the moment I'm putting on weight.

2 I want to .... smoking but I'm on 40 a day.

3 I want to .... more exercise but I haven't got time.

4 I want to .... my working hours but I have too much to do.

5 I want to .... more but my job is very stressful.

6 I want to .... on a diet because I'm overweight.

reduce
go
do
relax
lose
stop

Which of these are true for you? Do you want to do anything else to improve your health?

It's time to talk

Staying healthy can be difficult when you sit at work all day. But your organisation has given you €55,000 to spend on making your workplace healthier. Working in groups, discuss which of the following you should spend your money on.

Health action	Cost
Offer T'ai Chi classes to employees after work	€11,000
Buy exercise machines	€28,000
Employ a company nurse to give health checks	€23,500
Offer healthier food options in the canteen	€20,000
Book time for employees at the local swimming pool	€14,000
Employ a company masseur/se	€20,000
Employ a trainer for aerobic classes	€10,000

What is your decision?

Remember

When discussing opinions, remember to use these useful phrases.

Asking for opinions: What do you think we should do?
Do you think we should … ?

Giving an opinion: I think we should … / I don't think we should …
I agree. / I disagree.

On the agenda

Speaking
Organising things at work / Making small talk

Grammar
The present perfect

Pronunciation
Spelling and pronunciation

Anne Smithwick works as Personal Assistant to Jane Harrison. They work for a British sportswear manufacturer.

28 Perfect planning

Warm up

Have you learned something today? What?
Have you enjoyed work today? Why?
Have you pleased your boss today? When?

MONDAY	
TUESDAY	11 o'clock taxi to airport
WEDNESDAY	Italia Sports
THURSDAY	La Riviera – evening dinner
FRIDAY	Flight back at 16.00 – BA2357

Listen to this

Have you organised everything?

1 Listen to Anne and Jane talking about their visit to an exhibition in Sicily. Jane wants the latest news on the arrangements that Anne is making. Today is Monday and they are leaving tomorrow. Listen and correct the three mistakes on the diary page. ▶▶|28.1

2 Listen again. Are these sentences true or false? ▶▶|28.1

1 Anne has booked the Hilton Hotel.   **T** ☐ **F** ☐
2 Jane has never stayed in the Hilton.   **T** ☐ **F** ☐
3 Anne hasn't cancelled the meeting with Giulia yet.   **T** ☐ **F** ☐
4 Jane has never been to Sicily.   **T** ☐ **F** ☐

What do you think?   Do you have a PA? Would you like one? Why? What are PAs for?

Check your grammar

The present perfect

We can use the present perfect to talk about what has happened at work and at home. We can also use it to make small talk by talking about our experiences and what we have done in life. Complete the questions and answers below.

The present perfect uses the verb *to have* and the past participle.

Question	Positive	Negative
Have you (1) .... my flight?	I've booked it for the 17th.	But I (2) .... booked the hotel yet.
(3) .... she ever been to Madrid?	Yes, she's been several times.	But she hasn't (4) .... to Barcelona.

Now look at the way we use short answers.

Have you finished the report?	Yes, I (5)	No, I haven't.
Has she ever stayed at the Hilton?	Yes, she has.	No, she (6) ....

Grammar reference page 118 ▶▶▶

Do it yourself

1 Correct the mistakes in these sentences.

   1 I have done it last week.
   2 She haven't finished the report.
   3 Do you have been to Italy?
   4 I didn't have received any emails so far today.

2 Anne and her boss, Jane Harrison, meet during the exhibition. Complete their conversation with the correct form of the verb in the present perfect.

He hasn't heard the good news yet.

ANNE: I've got some good news for you. We (1) 've received (receive) three big new orders. Bob Martin of TXL (2) .... (order) our Apollo sports shoe.

JANE: That's excellent. How many (3) .... (order)?

ANNE: Three thousand. Great, isn't it! And ABC and Harcom Sports (4) .... (also / agree) to buy a thousand of our Eagle sports shirts.

JANE: Fantastic. (5) .... (you / tell) Peter yet? He'll be delighted.

ANNE: No, I (6) .... (not / tell) him yet. I'll phone him later this afternoon.

JANE: And (7) .... (you / speak to) any Japanese buyers?

ANNE: Yes, but no luck! In fact, we (8) .... (never / sell) any of our products in Japan. But, despite that, I have to say that the exhibition (9) .... (be) a great success.

JANE: Thanks very much, Anne.

Now listen and check. ▶▶|28.2

3 Look at Anne's checklist showing what she has and hasn't done. Then role-play a phone conversation between Anne and Jane. Make questions and answers like the example. Then changes roles.

Example: Confirm our lunch at Da Silvio's.   (Thursday at 1)

    " JANE: Have you confirmed our lunch at Da Silvio's?

    " ANNE: Yes, I have. I did it yesterday. The table is booked for Thursday at 1. "

Organise Jean-Luc meeting	next Friday ✔
Send Brenda Flanagan sales report	yesterday ✔
Send email to Rebecca	not yet ✗
Buy Jim a birthday present	bottle of whisky ✔
Water plants in office	not yet ✗

Test your partner   Write down a similar list of jobs you have done or have to do this week. Then give the list to your partner and answer his/her questions about which jobs you have done.

Spelling and pronunciation

1 How do you pronounce the two underlined words?

> Their rooms are very <u>comfortable</u>!

> Have you found the <u>receipt</u>?

Now listen and check. ▶▶|28.3

2 It is sometimes difficult to know how to pronounce words because the spelling doesn't always help you. Here are ten easily mispronounced words that have come up in this course. With a partner, decide on the correct pronunciation.

colleague	talked	budget
jewellery	weight	salmon
aisle	impatient	
castle	dessert	

Now listen and check. ▶▶|28.4

Make a note of words you find difficult to pronounce and review them regularly.

Test your partner Ask your partner to say a sentence with each of the words in the list. You have to say if the pronunciation is right or not.

It's time to talk

Remember that Jane asked Anne: 'Have you ever been to Sicily?'
The question 'Have you ever ...' is a useful way to make small talk. Look at this example.

Start by asking a question with the present perfect:

> A: Have you ever been to China?

Wait for a positive answer:

> B: Yes, I have.

Show interest and develop with the past simple:

> A: Really? When did you ... ? Where did you ... ? Why did you ... ?

Practise your small talk

Dinner talk

Work in pairs. You are having dinner with an important customer (your partner). Practise your small talk with short conversations using the questions below. Make your own questions, if you can.

Questions	Ideas
Travel: Have you ever been to ... ?	London / the USA / Asia ...
Work: Have you ever worked ... ?	in a factory / in sales / abroad ...
Sport: Have you ever been ... ?	scuba diving / mountain climbing ...
Food: Have you ever eaten ... ?	foie gras/ snake ...
Other: Have you ever ... ?	...

Remember

We can use the present perfect to talk about what has happened at work:
- Have you phoned TXL yet?
- We've received three big new orders.

We can also use it to make small talk:
- Have you ever been to Madrid?
- Have you ever worked abroad?

On the agenda

Speaking
Change

Communicating at work
Emails 3: Arranging meetings by email

Vocabulary
Describing change

Meet Frank Hatke. He works in sales for Bayer, the German chemicals company. Frank talks about changes in his organisation.

29 A changing world

Warm up

Frank works in sales. Would you like to work in sales? Why? Why not?

Read on

A year in Germany

1 We interviewed Frank about his work. Match our questions with Frank's answers.

1 Is it difficult to find work in eastern Germany at the moment?
2 Is the German economy healthy?
3 What do you do, Frank?
4 How was business last year?

Would you like to work in sales?

SALES

A
I work in Leverkusen, near Cologne, to help develop sales for the northern European part of our business. We've had many changes in the last few years and my work has increased a lot. But it's very interesting and I enjoy it.

B
Last year was a very good year for our company. We increased our sales and, more importantly, our market share went up a little, so we reached our target. The most important thing in business is to reach your target. But I have to say that competition in my business area is very strong now. You can see that with prices. Some of our product prices decreased a little last year.

Frank sells fertilisers to help farmers to grow food.

C
At the moment it is a bit difficult because of political questions. We now have the euro and I hope this will strengthen the economy in Germany. But prices have risen a lot. For example, petrol prices and typical supermarket goods are very high right now.

D
Yes, for many people. After the Wall came down a lot of factories closed in the eastern part, people lost their jobs and so unemployment went up a lot. I am from eastern Germany so I know about this problem. It's still difficult to find work and I think it will be a long time before we see unemployment go down.

2 Read the text again and find out what has happened to the following.

1 Unemployment in eastern Germany
2 The price of some of Frank's products
3 Bayer's market share
4 The amount of work Frank has to do

Bayer is based in Leverkusen.

What do you think?   Do you agree with Frank? He says: 'The most important thing in business is to reach your target.'

The words you need ... to talk about change

1 Match the sentences with the sales trends (a–e).

1 Sales went up a lot last month.
2 Sales have fallen gradually this year.
3 Turnover increased a little but then went down by €2 million.
4 Market share has stayed the same for the last few years.
5 Turnover decreased in the first quarter but went up by the end of the year.

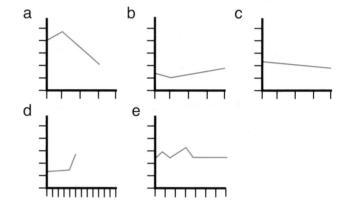

2 The tenses we use with the language of trends are very important.

Past years/months

We use the past simple: *Sales went up last month | last year | in January.*

Current year

If the year is not finished, we use the present perfect: *Sales have gone up this year.*

Complete the sentences with the correct form of the verb given.

1 Unemployment .... (decrease) by 5% last year.

2 Inflation .... (rise) by 2% so far this year.

3 Bank interest rates .... (fall) by 0.5% last month.

4 Taxes .... (increase) a lot already this year.

5 Petrol prices .... (go up) by 20 cents in July.

It's time to talk

We can describe increases and decreases like this:

	Subject	Up/down	How big	When
Past simple	Sales	decreased	a little	last year.
Present perfect	Business/Sales	has/have increased	a lot	this year.

Now work with a partner and use the table to help you describe important changes in:

• your organisation last year
• your country.

Were the changes good or bad?

Communicating at work

Emails 3: Arranging meetings by email

1 Amanda wants to arrange meetings with four colleagues. Match up Amanda's emails with their replies.

1 Hi, can we meet next Monday at 8 o'clock?
2 Are you free next Tuesday for a meeting?
3 Would Wednesday be convenient for a meeting? Say 2 o'clock?
4 Could we fix a meeting for Thursday? How about 10 in your office?

a That's fine. But could we make it 2.30 instead?
b Fine, my office then. Will you send an agenda?
c Sorry, I've got a meeting at 8.15 with Simon. How about 9.30 instead?
d I'm afraid not. I'm on holiday next week. I'll call you when I get back. Is that OK?

2 Complete the sentences about arranging meetings by email with words from the list.

| can't |
| by |
| forward |
| meet |
| make |

Suggesting

Could we arrange a meeting for 10 on Monday?

Can we (1) .... on Monday at 10?

Would Monday at 10 be convenient for a meeting?

Could you let me know (2) .... the end of today?

Accepting

Monday's OK.

Fine, my office.

Look (3) .... to seeing you.

Rearranging

Sorry, I'm busy on Monday.

I'm afraid I (4) .... I'm not in the office.

Could we (5) .... it Tuesday instead?

But could we say Tuesday?

3 Now it's time to practise. Work with a partner.

- Write a short email to your partner to fix a meeting. Then give it to your partner.
- Reply to the email which you receive. Ask to rearrange the meeting. Then give your email to your partner.
- Reply to the email which asks to rearrange a meeting.

Finally, read out one of your emails in class. Who is the best emailer?

Remember

When arranging meetings by email, remember to:
- specify the time, date and place clearly
- refer to any attachments you are sending
- confirm when you receive documentation for the meeting.

On the agenda

Speaking
Continuing your learning

Social phrases
Saying goodbye

Vocabulary
Learning for life

Meet Gayle Martz and her dog Sherpa. Find out how Gayle changed her lifestyle.

Warm up

Which of these people's lifestyles would you most/least like to have? Why?
- A peace-keeping soldier
- An artist
- An actor
- A professional cyclist
- A teacher

30 Jets and pets

Listen to this

Working with animals

1 We interviewed Gayle Martz. Listen to her talking about her business and her lifestyle. Are these sentences true or false? ▶▶|30.1

It's all thanks to Gayle.

    1 Gayle has a company which sells pet carriers.   T ☐ F ☐

    2 She started the company in 1990.   T ☐ F ☐

    3 She's from New York.   T ☐ F ☐

    4 She eats a lot of vegetarian food.   T ☐ F ☐

2 Listen again and answer these questions. ▶▶|30.1

    1 How did Gayle get the idea for her company?

    2 How much is Gayle's company now worth?

    3 What does Gayle always try to be?

    4 What does she do to relax?

What do you think?   Do you have a good work–life balance? Would you like to change your life like Gayle Martz? Why? Why not? Gayle says: 'We are learning things all through our life and I always try to be a good learner.' Are you a good learner?

The techniques you need ... for learning vocabulary

During this course you have learned a lot of new words. You have also studied ideas about how to learn words. Now – at the end of the course – it is important to review some of these ideas and make a personal learning plan for the future.

1 **Group words and expressions under themes.** It makes them easier to remember.
Match the words and expressions in the boxes to the correct subject.

Work ☐

Internet ☐

Health ☐

A	**B**	**C**
download	fresh food	manager
surf	do yoga	I'm in charge of ...
website	I'm not very fit	salary
online	lose weight	I have my own business

2 **Learn the verbs and nouns which go together.** It makes your English more correct. Match each group of verbs (1–4) with a noun in the box.

1 fix / organise / have / cancel ....

2 have / spend / save / lend ....

3 send / write / read / delete ....

4 have / drive / park / crash ....

> a car
>
> a meeting
>
> money
>
> emails

3 **Learn word families and how to use each word.** It helps to build sentences. Which word in the box completes each sentence?

Noun	organisation
Verb	organise
Adjective	organised

1 I am very well ....

2 It's a very big ....

3 I .... training seminars for our sales staff.

'I always try to be a good learner.'

It's time to talk

Choose ideas from the action list and create an action plan to learn words in the future. Discuss your ideas with your partner.

 Actions to build vocabulary

 Get a good dictionary

 Read – to consolidate and meet new words

 Go to more English classes

 Write in English every week

 Listen to English cassettes/CDs every week

 Test yourself regularly

Speak English as much as you can

We all have our own ways of learning vocabulary.

Review the words you know for 10 minutes every day.

My action plan

1 _____

2 _____

3 _____

4 _____

5 _____

Saying goodbye

1 Complete the dialogues with phrases (a–j) below.

Organising airport transport

A: Linda, when are you leaving?
B: I've ordered a taxi for 1 o'clock.
A: I'm leaving the office early.
(1) ...., if you want.
B: (2) .... but I can take a taxi.
It's no problem.

Exchanging contact information

A: (3) ....
B: Oh, thanks, I'm afraid I don't have one with me.
A: Don't worry.
B: But (4) .... and email address.
A: Great. (5) .... on Monday with the information you want.

Giving a present

A: Before you go, (6) ....
B: What's this?
A: (7) .... to say thank you.
B: It's beautiful. Thank you very much.
A: (8) .... Thank you.

Saying goodbye

B: I have to go. The taxi's here.
A: Well, (9) ....
B: Yes, the same for me. It was great.
A: Have a good trip back.
B: See you soon, I hope.
A: (10) .... Bye.

a it was nice working with you	**f**	this is for you
b Take care	**g**	I'll contact you
c I can take you to the airport	**h**	Here's my business card
d That's very kind	**i**	It's a little present
e My pleasure	**j**	this is my mobile number

2 Now listen and check. ▶▶30.2

3 Practise reading the dialogues with a partner.

Have a go

Cover the dialogues above and make your own, starting with the words below.

Organising airport transport

When ...

Exchanging contact information

Here's my ...

Giving a present

Before you ...

Saying goodbye

I have to ...

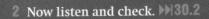

Remember

Learning a language is hard at first but it gets easier. Little but often is best. Can you do English for 20 minutes every day?

Enjoy your English.

Good luck!

Revision 2 Units 16–30

Grammar

1 Catherine Wilson is talking to Brian Corrigan at a conference in Edinburgh. Look at Brian's answers and write the questions Catherine asked.

1 ....
   I'm a trainer. I teach project management.

2 ....
   I'm staying at the Marriott Hotel.

3 ....
   We're having dinner at an Indian restaurant at about 8.

4 ....
   Yes, I have. A long time ago. It's a great city.

5 ....
   About 1983.

2 Compete the sales report using the past simple or the present perfect.

> **Sales report**
>
> This year is a good year for D&D so far. Overall sales
> (1) .... (increase) by 10%. This is mainly
> because our business in China (2) .... (rise) by
> 12%. This is much better than last year when sales (3)
> .... (fall) by 2%. In America there has been no
> change: so far we (4) .... (stay) at the same level
> as the previous year. The best thing is the share price
> which (5) .... (go up) in value by 10%. This is
> better than in May when share prices
> (6) .... (go down) by 5%.

3 Choose the correct answer to complete the conversation between two salespeople at a trade fair in Hanover.

A: So, are you planning to stay in Hanover for the weekend?

B: No, I don't have (1) *much/many* time. I'm just here for the exhibition.

A: I see. Are you meeting many customers here?

B: No, generally, we only meet (2) *a few/a little* customers here.

A: Do you get (3) *much/many* orders after your Hanover visit?

B: Yes, usually. It can generate a lot of business.

4 Complete these tips about language learning with the correct word or phrase from the box.

don't have to	have to	should

1 You (1) .... try to learn a few words every day. This is important.

2 You (2) .... speak a language as much as possible if you want to learn it.

3 You (3) .... study for five hours every day. Twenty minutes every day is enough.

General vocabulary

1 Choose the correct answer to complete the sentences.

1 Pork, beef and lamb are all examples of *meal/meat*.

2 Another word for a sweet is *a desert/a dessert*.

3 Steak and kidney pie is a classic English *dish/plate*.

4 You order wine from the *wine list/wine menu*.

5 After the starter, you eat the *main meal/main course*.

6 When you are ready to pay, you ask for the *bill/receipt*.

2 Complete the sentences with the correct verb from the box.

save	lend	get
spend	borrow	pay

1 I .... a lot of money on CDs.

2 You can .... a lot of money by shopping in the sales.

3 Could I .... €10, please. I forgot my wallet.

4 Could you .... me €10, please. I forgot my wallet.

5 I'll .... you back later, I promise!

6 I have to .... some money out from a cash machine.

Business communication

1 Complete the missing words in the email.

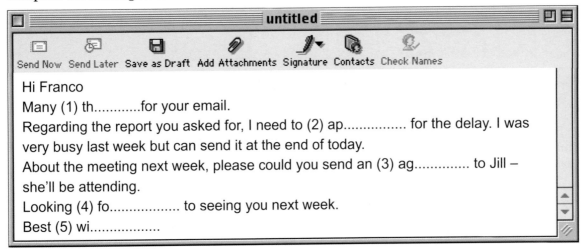

```
☐ ▭▭▭▭▭▭▭▭▭▭▭▭ untitled ▭▭▭▭▭▭▭▭▭▭▭▭ 🖭 🗏
      ▭           ▭           🖬           📎           ✒▾        🗐         ✐
  Send Now   Send Later   Save as Draft   Add Attachments   Signature   Contacts   Check Names

  Hi Franco
  Many (1) th............for your email.
  Regarding the report you asked for, I need to (2) ap................ for the delay. I was
  very busy last week but can send it at the end of today.
  About the meeting next week, please could you send an (3) ag.............. to Jill –
  she'll be attending.
  Looking (4) fo................. to seeing you next week.
  Best (5) wi.................
```

2 Choose the correct answer to complete the phone conversation.

ANGEL: Sam, can we (1) *make/fix* a meeting for next week? I'd like to (2) *discuss/talk* the personnel plan for next year.

SAM: Sure, no problem. When is (3) *comfortable/convenient* for you?

ANGEL: Well, (4) *what/what's* about next Thursday at 10 o'clock?

SAM: Fine. Can you send me an email to (5) *confirm/repeat* that?

ANGEL: OK, I can do that. So, (6) *speak/see* you on Thursday next week. Bye.

SAM: Yes, bye.

Pronunciation

1 Listen and write down the ten numbers and prices which you hear. ▶▶R2.1

1 ....
2 ....
3 ....
4 ....
5 ....
6 ....
7 ....
8 ....
9 ....
10 ....

2 Listen to this conversation and mark the main stress in these sentences. ▶▶R2.2

A: Are you staying for two or three days?

B: I'm planning to stay for three days.

A: Where are you staying?

B: I'm staying at Vanna's house.

A: Have you been to Italy before?

B: I've been lots of times before!

Business vocabulary

1 Put the letters in the correct order.

1 Another word for total sales

runtrove ....

2 Money your organisation spends to do business

scots ....

3 The name of the main department in a company which deals with money

ninefac ....

4 An amount of money which you can spend in a department, on training, for example

dugbet ....

5 The opposite of *loss*

fiptor ....

6 The difference between the total production cost of a product and the sales price

raming ....

Social phrases

1 Match the questions (1–6) with the correct response (a–f).

1 Can you show me where the meeting room is?
2 I'd like a wake-up call in the morning.
3 Is there a cash point near here?
4 Can you recommend somewhere to eat?
5 Are you free for lunch on Tuesday?
6 Could I borrow £10 until tomorrow?

a Yes, I am.
b Yes, there's a bank opposite the hotel.
c No problem.
d Of course. Follow me.
e Certainly. What time?
f I know an excellent Chinese.

2 Annette is saying goodbye to Ian after a successful business meeting. Put the sentences in the correct order.

☐1 A: Right, I must go. My taxi is outside.

☐ B: My pleasure.

☐ A: Take care. See you next month.

☐ B: Before you go, Annette, this is a little present just to say thank you.

☐ A: I shall eat these on the plane. OK, Ian, thank you again for everything.

☐ B: Yes. Have a good trip. Bye.

☐ A: Oh, my favourite chocolates. Thank you very much.

☐ B: No problem. It was good to have you here.

☐9 A: Thank you. Bye.

File cards

2 Helping people to learn

Communicating at work

3

STUDENT A

Call 1: Phone Student B and ask him/her to email you a copy of the new sales report.

Call 2: Student B phones you. Tell him/her that the management meeting next week is at 12.00 on Thursday.

5 Health care – public or private?

Communicating at work

Could you spell that, please?

STUDENT A

Ask your partner to write down these abbreviations:

PA   EU   CNN   CIA   JIT

Check that he/she writes them down correctly.
Do you or your partner know what they mean?

Key to abbreviations
Personal Assistant
European Union
Cable Network News
Central Intelligence Agency
Just in Time

5 Health care – public or private?

Communicating at work

Can I take a message?

STUDENT A

Call 1: Your name is Peter Wenk. You work for Zurich International Life Assurance. Your number is 00 41 1 4473322511. Call Florence Villemain to tell her that you are free on Friday morning from 9 to 11 o'clock.

Call 2: You work in the same office in Turin as Luigi Eranio. He is out of the office all day. Take a phone message for him and get the caller's name and number.

7 Changing workspace

It's time to talk

STUDENT A

Look at the information below and answer your partner's questions.

Office 1
The building

Individual offices (yes – not open plan)

Car park (yes, but small)

Staff restaurant (yes, excellent)

Swimming pool (no)

Smoking room (yes – one smoking room on each floor)

The area

Railway station (no, but bus station)

Shops (some – not a lot)

Fitness centre (yes, open to the public)

Banks (yes, two)

Restaurants (yes, but only one – a good Italian restaurant)

There are 1,500 square metres of space.

10 Eating around the world

It's time to talk

STUDENT A

You prefer London. You know it very well because you have a holiday there every year. Prepare some reasons for your choice and then discuss them with your colleagues.

14 Médecins Sans Frontières

It's time to talk

STUDENT A

1 You work for the Johnson Corporation. Be prepared to use the information below to answer Student B's questions.

2 Prepare some questions to ask Student B about his/her organisation.

3 Now interview Student B and complete the table on page 49.

Name	Johnson Corporation
When started	1949
Head office	Chicago, USA
Locations	Chicago; and two factories – one near Chicago, the other outside Mexico City, Mexico
Main activities	Manufacturing paints for the car industry
Other information	2,300 employees in total; 1,200 in Mexico. Business this year is good. The company wants to set up a factory in China next year.

16 Project Stockholm

It's time to talk

STUDENT A

Job	Engineer
Company	DeltaCom
Hotel	Hilton
Current project	Building a new subway line from Heathrow airport to the centre of London. You are not enjoying things because you are having some technical problems.

19 Living in Hong Kong

It's time to talk

STUDENT A

You are travelling to a trade fair in Tokyo, Japan. Telephone the trade fair organiser (Student B) and ask for some travel information and about the culture of Japan. Use the information below.

Travel information

You want to know if:

- you have to get a visa to travel to Japan
- you have to buy a special mobile phone
- you should take traveller's cheques
- you should leave tips in restaurants

Cultural information

You want to know if:

- you should use first names or not with business contacts
- you have to arrive on time for meetings
- you should wear casual clothes at business meetings
- you have to shake hands with people every time you meet them

22 Working for Rolls Royce

STUDENT A

You receive this email from your boss.

> Please could you call Jean Zidance and ask for the following information? I need to know asap.
> 1 Berlin exhibition
>   Number of sales people from our company going to the exhibition
>   Amount of exhibition space we have – 5m^2 or 15m^2?
> 2 Sales
>   Number of new orders last month
>   Amount of money we spent on marketing last month
> 3 Travel
>   Number of days of foreign travel planned for next year.
>
> Regards
> Martine Hugot

Plan the questions you need to ask Jean Zidance. Then call Jean Zidance (Student B) and get the information.

25 Driving to Romania

It's time to talk

STUDENT A

You work with Anna Harland. Student B works with Simone Triquet. You need to arrange a management meeting early next week to discuss a trip to Poland. It is necessary to have a minimum of three people at management meetings. Look at your desk diaries below. Call Student B and arrange a time when THREE of you can meet.

Remember to use the present continuous.

		You	Anna	Student B	Simone
MON	am	am Travel to HQ to do job interviews	am	am	am
	pm	pm	pm Travel to Berlin for conference	pm	pm
TUES	am	am	am	am	am
	pm	pm	pm Meet Paolo Vierri	pm	pm
WED	am	am Customer visit	am	am	am
	pm	pm	pm Leave work early – go to doctor	pm	pm

26 Out of order

It's time to talk

STUDENT A

Imagine you have these problems.

- One of my customers always smokes in my office when he visits.
- My boss always arrives ten minutes late for our meetings.
- The coffee from the drinks machine tastes terrible.
- I work 60 hours a week. I don't have enough time for my family.
- My most important customer sends me too many emails. I get 20 or more from him every day.

Tell your partner your problems. Can he/she solve them for you?

2 Helping people to learn

Communicating at work

3

STUDENT B

Call 1: Student A phones you. Tell him/her you can email a copy of the new sales report today.

Call 2: Phone Student A and ask him/her for the time of the management meeting next week.

5 Health care – public or private?

Communicating at work

Could you spell that, please?

STUDENT B

Ask your partner to write down these abbreviations:

VP   VIP   HR   WTO   PR

Check that he/she writes them down correctly.

Do you or your partner know what they mean?

Key to abbreviations
Vice President
Very Important Person
Human Resources
World Trade Organisation
Public Relations

5 Health care – public or private?

Communicating at work

Can I take a message?

STUDENT B

Call 1: You work in the same office in Paris as Florence Villemain. She is out of the office all day. Take a phone message for her and get the caller's name and number.

Call 2: Your name is Elizabeth Davidsen. You work for Norsoft in Oslo. Your number is 00 47 88776655. Call Luigi Eranio to tell him that the report is fine.

7 Changing workspace

It's time to talk

STUDENT B

Look at the information below and answer your partner's questions.

Office 2
The building

Individual offices (no – open plan)

Car park (yes, very large car park)

Staff restaurant (yes, small but good menu)

Swimming pool (no)

Smoking room (no – no-smoking building)

The area

Railway station (yes)

Shops (yes, big shopping centre)

Fitness centre (yes, you must be a member)

Banks (only one)

Restaurants (some – not a lot)

There are 2,500 square metres of space.

10 Eating around the world

It's time to talk

STUDENT B

You prefer Rome because the food and weather are better. Prepare some reasons for your choice and then discuss them with your colleagues.

14 Médecins Sans Frontières

It's time to talk

STUDENT B

1 You work for Globalreach. Be prepared to use the information below to answer Student A's questions.

2 Prepare some questions to ask Student A about his/her organisation.

3 Now interview Student A and complete the table on page 49.

Name	Globalreach
When started	1991
Head office	Paris
Locations	Paris, London, Frankfurt, New York
Main activities	Marketing consultants for major global companies
Other information	185 employees. Turnover of $150 million. Business is difficult but things should improve next year.

16 Project Stockholm

It's time to talk

STUDENT B

Job	Marketing manager
Company	Kamen Records
Hotel	Sheraton
Current project	Creating a website for selling music directly on the Internet. The schedule is to finish at the end of next year. Everything is going well at the moment.

19 Living in Hong Kong

It's time to talk

STUDENT B

Student A is travelling to a trade fair in Tokyo, Japan. You are the trade fair organiser. Student A will telephone you and ask you for some travel information and about the culture of Japan. Answer his/her questions with the information below.

<u>Travel information</u>

VISA You have to apply for a visa. Contact your local Japanese embassy.

MOBILE PHONE   You don't know anything about the mobile phone network. Recommend that Student A contacts his/her mobile phone operator.

MONEY Traveller's cheques are a good idea because they are safe.

EATING OUT Leave a 10% tip in restaurants.

<u>Cultural information</u>

NAMES In Japan you should use surnames with business contacts.

TIME It is absolutely necessary to be on time for meetings.

DRESS Dress smartly at all times.

HANDSHAKES The Japanese use the western handshake but often prefer to bow. Do not shake hands after the first contact in the morning.

22 Working for Rolls Royce

It's time to talk

STUDENT B

You are Jean Zidance. Your partner will phone you to ask for this information. Plan your answers to his/her questions.

1 <u>Berlin exhibition planning</u> 23 sales people from our company will go to the exhibition.

   We have 15m^2 exhibition space.

2 <u>Sales figures</u>   54 new orders last month.

   Last month's marketing costs were €34,000.

3 <u>Travel</u> Estimated number of days of foreign travel next year: 14.

25 Driving to Romania

It's time to talk

STUDENT B

You work with Simone Triquet. Student A works with Anna Harland. Student A will call you about arranging a management meeting early next week to discuss a trip to Poland. It is necessary to have a minimum of three people at management meetings. Look at your desk diaries below. Arrange a time when THREE of you can meet.

Remember to use the present continuous.

		Student A	Anna	You	Simone
MON	am	am	am	am Meet Sacha Daligault at airport	am – meeting all day
	pm	pm	pm	pm English training course: 3 hours	pm
TUES	am	am	am	am Customer visit new employees	am Run training seminar for
	pm	pm	pm	pm Golf with Ingrid	pm
WED	am	am	am	am	am
	pm	pm	pm	pm Present new budget to board	pm

26 Out of order

It's time to talk

STUDENT B

Imagine you have these problems.

- My colleagues are too noisy. I can't get any work done.
- I have to travel abroad a lot but I hate flying.
- I spend too much time worrying about work.
- My boss keeps giving me more work and I never manage to catch up. It's just getting worse and worse.
- I'm in love with my colleague but I'm too shy to tell him/her.

Tell your partner your problems. Can he/she solve them for you?

4 North and south

It's time to talk

The stress check (page 20)

Score

40–50	Excellent (you are in control)
35–39	Good (but could be better)
30–34	OK (work less)
29 or less	Danger! (get some help)

10 Eating around the world

It's time to talk

STUDENT C

You strongly prefer Paris because you love French culture and French food. Prepare some reasons for your choice and then discuss them with your colleagues.

24 I buy money

It's time to talk

Are you good with money? (page 82)

Analysis

- If you chose 1, 2, 6 or 8, you are a person who is very careful with money. But if you didn't choose 3 or 7, some people will think you are mean!
- If you chose 4, 5 or 9, you are probably not very good with money and may like to spend too much too quickly! Perhaps you need to be more careful.
- If you chose 3 or 7, you are probably a very generous person.
- Most people probably choose a balance of the above – to spend a little, save a little and give a little. In our opinion, balance is the most sensible option!

25 Driving to Romania

Do it yourself

3

1 Participants

Anna Parkland + Harald Henrikssen – Coming
Johan Meier – Not coming, too busy

2 Speakers

Confirmed programme:

Tues 10.00	Jessica Langer talking about Quality Management
Wed 09.00	Thomas Salter talking about Selling
	No confirmation from other speakers

3 Evening programme

Tues evening	Go to opera
Wed evening	See a Shakespeare play at Stratford

Grammar reference

Index

Grammar reference

The present simple tense (Units 1 and 4)

In *English365* Book 1 we look at how we can use the present simple to ask and answer questions when we meet people (see Unit 1).

Where do you live?
I live in London but I come from Dublin originally.
Who do you work for?
I'm with IBM.

We also look at how we can use it to talk about everyday routines (see Unit 4).

The verb *to be*

Positive			Contractions
I	am		I'm
You	are		You're
He		a hard worker.	He's
She	is		She's
It			It's
We			We're
You	are	hard workers.	You're
They			They're

Questions	
Am I	
Is he	
Is she	
Is it	free on Saturday?
Are you	
Are we	
Are they	

Negative			Contractions
I	am not		I'm not
You	are not		You're not / You aren't
We	are not	happy with this.	We're not / We aren't
He			He's not / he isn't
She	is not		She's not / she isn't
It			It's not / It isn't

Short answers	Contractions
Yes, I am.	
Yes, you/we/they are.	
Yes, he/she/it is.	
No, I am not.	No, I'm not.
No, you/we/they are not.	No, you/we/they aren't.
No, he/she/it is not.	No, he isn't.

Other verbs

Positive			Negative			Contractions
I			I			I don't like
You	start		You	do not like		You don't like
We			We			We don't like
They		work at 8.	They		writing reports.	They don't like
He			He			He doesn't like
She	starts		She	does not like		She doesn't like
It			It			It doesn't like

Questions

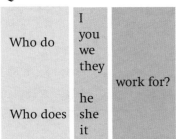

Spellings

For most verbs: add -s for the *he/she/it* form.
For verbs ending in -s, -sh, -ch, -x: add -es.
Note also: *have* → *has, do* → *does, go* → *goes.*

Yes/no questions

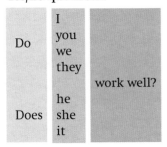

Short answers

Yes, I/you/we/they do.
Yes, he/she/it does.

No, I/you/we/they do not.
No he/she/it doesn't.

Contractions

No, I/you/we/they don't.
No, he/she/it doesn't.

Have and *have got*

There are two ways to use the verb *to have*.

Have

We can use this in the same way as the present simple:

She has an interesting job.
Do you have my mobile number?
I don't have much time.

Have got

Positive

| I You We They | have got | a big house in Barcelona. |
| He She It | has got | |

Contractions

I've got
You've got
We've got
They've got

He's got
She's got
It's got

Questions

| Have | I you we they | got a pen? |
| Has | he she it | |

Negative

| I You We They | have not got | much time. |
| He She It | has not got | |

Contractions

I haven't got
You haven't got
We haven't got
They haven't got

He hasn't got
She hasn't got
It hasn't got

Short answers

Yes, I/you/we/they have.
Yes, he/she/it has.

No, I/you/we/they have not.
No, he/she/it has not.

Contractions

No, I/you/we/they haven't.
No, he/she/it hasn't.

Time adverbs and expressions with the present simple tense (Unit 4)

In *English365* Book 1, we look at how we can use the present simple with time adverbs and expressions to talk about things we do regularly at work and/or at home.

> I go to Berlin about **three times a year**.
> I **usually** go in the spring, in the summer and just before Christmas.
> I **never** go to Paris in the spring. I **sometimes** go in the summer.

Time adverbs

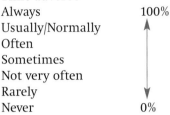

Always	100%
Usually/Normally	
Often	
Sometimes	
Not very often	
Rarely	
Never	0%

Short answers

Do you ever work at the weekend?
- Yes, sometimes.
- Yes, occasionally.
- No, never.

Time expressions

Once a day / a week / a month / a year (x 1)
Twice a day / a week / a month / a year (x 2)
Three times a day / a week / a month / a year (x 3)
Several times a day / a week / a month / a year
All the time

Questions with *How often ... ?*

How often do you work late?
How often do you get to the office before 8 o'clock?

There is / *There are* with *some*, *any* and *a lot of* (Unit 7)

In *English365* Book 1 we look at how we can use *There is* / *There are* with countable nouns and uncountable nouns to describe where we work.

	Countable singular	Countable plural	Uncountable nouns
Positive	There's a restaurant. There's an open office.	There are some table games.	There's some information on the new database.
Negative	There isn't a fixed desk. There isn't an exercise room. There's no problem.	There aren't any personal offices. There are no personal offices.	There isn't any paper. There's no paper.
Question	Is there a restaurant? Is there a swimming pool?	Are there any places to work in private?	Is there any personal space?
Answer	Yes, there is. No, there isn't.	Yes, there are. No, there aren't.	Yes, there is. No, there isn't.

We often use *some* in positives and *any* in negatives and questions. But we also use *some* when we ask for or offer something.

> Can I have some water?
> Would you like some coffee?

We can use *a lot of* in positives, negatives and questions with countable plural nouns and uncountable nouns.

> There are a lot of problems with this.
> There isn't a lot of time to solve them.

Some common uncountable nouns	
advice	news
English	time
furniture	traffic
information	travel
luggage	weather
money	work

Comparative and superlative adjectives (Unit 10)

In *English365* Book 1 we look at how we can compare people and things using the comparative and superlative forms of adjectives.

Comparatives
> Hans is taller than me.
> Lisa works harder than anyone.
> I think the film is better than the book.

Superlatives
> Hans is the tallest guy in the office.
> Lisa is the most efficient person in the whole organisation.

Comparative and superlative adjectives

Rule	Adjective	Comparative	Superlative
One syllable: add *-er/-est*	cheap	cheaper	cheapest
Two syllables ending in 'y': change 'y' to 'i' and add *-er/-est*	tasty	tastier	tastiest
Most other two syllable adjectives*: use *more/less* and *most/least*	modern	more/less modern	most/least modern
Three or more syllables: use *more/less* and *most/least*	expensive	more/less expensive	most/least expensive
Learn the irregular adjectives	good bad	better worse	best worst
*Some two syllable adjectives take *-er/-est* Some can take both forms	quiet polite	quieter politer more/less polite	quietest politest more/least polite

If you are not sure, use a dictionary.

The past simple tense (Unit 13)

In *English365* Book 1 we look at how we can use the past simple to talk about our past life and past events.

I saw her at the meeting last week.
I worked for Siemens from 1990 to 1995. Now I work for myself.
Where did you go to school? What did you do then?
When I was young I lived in Jamaica. Then we moved to Miami and I got a job in a travel agency.

With *ago*:
*I left the company three months **ago**.*

The verb *to be*

Positive

I He She It	was	in the office all day yesterday.
You We They	were	

Negative

I He She It	was not	in the office last week.
You We They	were not	

Contractions

wasn't

weren't

Questions

Was	I he she it	still there at 7?
Were	we you they	

Short answers

Yes, I/he/she/it was.
Yes, we/you/they were.

No, I/he/she/it/ was not.
No, we/you/they were not.

Contractions

No, I/he/she/it wasn't.
No, we/you/they weren't.

Other verbs

Positive
Add *–ed* to the infinitive form of the verb.

I You He She It We They	joined the company in 1995.

Negative
Use *didn't* and the infinitive of the verb.

I You He She It We They	didn't enjoy it at first.

Questions
Use *did* and the infinitive of the verb.

Did	I you he she it we they	do a good job?

Short answers

Yes, I did.   No, I didn't.

Some time phrases with the past simple
Last weekend
At 9 this morning
On Thursday
This morning
In 1993
In September
50 years ago

For the forms of irregular verbs, see page 119.

The present continuous tense (Units 16 and 25)

We can use the present continuous tense in three important ways to talk about temporary actions, with the focus on the present moment (see Unit 16).

At the moment
She's not working today.
He's writing the report.

Current projects/situations
I'm working on the new budget.
She's managing the whole team.
They're building a new bridge over the river.

Current changes/developments
Life is getting more difficult.
People are working harder than before.
We are taking more holidays.

The present continuous is also useful when you talk about fixed future plans (see Unit 25).

What are you doing this evening?
We're having some people to dinner.
I'm playing cards with my friends.
I'm working late.

Where are you going on holiday?
We're renting a villa in Turkey.
We're having a beach holiday in Jamaica.

Are they meeting him on Tuesday?
No, they're seeing him on Wednesday morning.

Positive		Contractions		Questions	
I am		I'm		Am I	
You are		You're		Are you	
We are		We're		Are we	
They are	having lunch.	They're		Are they	having a good time?
He is		He's		Is he	
She is		She's		Is she	
It is		It's		Is it	

Negative		Contractions	Short answers	Contractions
I am not		I'm not	Yes, I am.	
You are not		You're not / You aren't	Yes, you/we/they are.	
We are not		We're not / We aren't	Yes, he/she/it is.	
They are not	doing any overtime this week.	They're not / They aren't		
He is not		He's not / He isn't	No, I am not.	No, I'm not.
She is not		She's not / She isn't	No, you/we/they are not.	No, you/we/they aren't.
It is not		It's not / It isn't	No, he/she/it is not.	No, he/she/it isn't.

Verbs not usually in the continuous form

Some verbs do not usually have a continuous form.

For thinking and feeling

Believe	I believe he's in Japan at the moment.
Know	They know that she's coming today.
Understand	I'm sorry, I don't understand.
Remember	Do you remember that hotel in London?

For possession

Belong	This book belongs to Jimmy Dutton.
Have	Do you have any red shirts?
Own	He owns half the island.

For the senses

Smell	It smells awful.
Taste	But it tastes delicious.
Sound	It sounds OK.

For wants and likes

Like	I like it here.
Love	I love you more than I say.
Hate	She hates the winter.
Need	I need you so much.
Prefer	He prefers cross-country to downhill skiing.
Wish	I wish I could fly.

For how things look or seem

Look	It looks absolutely great.
Seem	It seems OK.

Others

Matter	It doesn't matter.
Depend	It depends on the weather.
Hear	I hear that you're getting married.
Owe	He owes me $100.

Should and *have to* (Unit 19)

Should

We can use *should* when we want to recommend something.

> *You should try the cheese. It's delicious.*
> *You should stop seeing him.*

Positive and negative

We use *should* + infinitive without *to*.

I You We They He She It	should shouldn't	do it.

Have to

We can use *have to* when we talk about rules that somebody else has made.

> *You have to go outside to smoke.*
> *I have to get up very early tomorrow.*
> *We all have to go to the meeting and we have to be there on time.*

We use *don't have to* when there is no obligation to do something.

> *You don't have to finish it tonight.*
> *We'd like you to wear it but you don't have to.*
> *You don't have to stay late if you don't want to.*

We use *have to* + infinitive without *to*.

Positive

I You We They	have to	leave at 9.
He She It	has to	

Negative

I You We They	don't have to	go.
He She It	doesn't have to	

Questions

Do	I you we they	have to	be there?
Does	he she it	have to	

Many, much, a few, a little (Unit 22)

In *English365* Book 1 we look at how we can use *many*, *much*, *a few* and *a little* to talk about quantity.

Many

With countable nouns, mainly in questions and negatives:

> *He doesn't have many friends.*
> *Do many people know about this?*
> *How many people know about it?*

Much

With uncountable nouns, mainly in questions and negatives:

> *I don't have much time.*
> *Is there much interest in this?*
> *How much information do you need?*

A few

With countable nouns, mainly in positives and questions:

> *There were only a few people at his presentation.*
> *Could you give me a few more ideas?*

A little

With uncountable nouns, mainly in positives and questions:

> *I get by with a little help from my friends.*
> *Can you give me a little more information?*

See Unit 7 for information on *a lot of*.

The present perfect tense (Unit 28)

In *English365* Book 1 we look at how we can use the present perfect to talk about what has happened at work or at home.

> *I've booked the tickets for your trip to Prague.*
> *Have you called the hotel?*
> *No, I haven't. I haven't had time.*

We also look at how we can use it to make small talk.

> *Have you ever been to New England in the autumn?*
> *No, I haven't. I've travelled a lot but I've never been to the States.*

We use *have* + the past participle of the verb (see page 120 for a list of irregular verbs).

Positive

I You We They	have		finished the report.	**Contractions** I've You've We've They've
He She (It)	has	not		He's She's It's

Negative

I We They	You have		told her about it.	**Contractions** I haven't You haven't We haven't They haven't
He She (It)	has	not		He hasn't She hasn't It hasn't

Questions

Have	I you we they	called him today?
Has	he she (it)	

Short answers

Yes, I/you/we/they have.
Yes, he/she/it/ hasn't.

No, I/you/we/they have not.
No, he/she/it has not.

Contractions

No, I/you/we/they haven't
No, he/she/it hasn't.

Personal pronouns and adjectives

Subject pronouns

I
You
He
She
It
We
They

I like the new sales manager. She's fun.
We have lunch at 1 o'clock.
They want more money.

Object pronouns

Me
You
Him
Her
It
Us
Them

The new sales manager doesn't like me.
Look at them!
Tell him to stop it.

Possessive adjectives

My
Your
His
Her
Its
Our
Your
Their

He's using my cup.
You need to take your coat.
The company is going to change its logo.

Question words

Who do you work for?	I work for Peka Systems.
Where do you live?	I live in Switzerland.
What do you do?	I'm an engineer.
Why did you join this company?	Because it has a good product range.
When did you start with Peka?	In 1990.
Which country do you visit most?	France.
Whose company is it?	It belongs to a man called Peter Weber.
How did he become the owner?	It was his father's company.
How far is it from your home to your office?	About 20 kilometres.
How often do you travel abroad?	Usually about once a month.
How many people work for Peka?	About 140.
How much do you earn?	I can't tell you that!

Irregular verbs

Infinitive	Past simple	Past participle
be	was/were	been
become	became	become
begin	began	begun
break	broke	broken
bring	brought	brought
build	built	built
buy	bought	bought
choose	chose	chosen
come	came	came
cost	cost	cost
cut	cut	cut
do	did	done
drink	drank	drunk
drive	drove	driven
eat	ate	eaten
fall	felt	felt
feel	felt	felt
find	found	found
forget	forgot	forgotten
fly	flew	flown
get	got	got
give	gave	given
go	went	gone
grow	grew	grown
have	had	had
hear	heard	heard
hit	hit	hit
hold	held	held
hurt	hurt	hurt
keep	kept	kept
know	knew	known
lead	led	led

Infinitive	Past simple	Past participle
learn	learnt	learnt
leave	left	left
lend	lent	lent
lie	lay	lain
make	made	made
mean	meant	meant
meet	met	met
pay	paid	paid
put	put	put
read	read	read
rise	rose	risen
run	run	run
say	said	said
see	saw	seen
sell	sold	sold
send	sent	sent
shut	shut	shut
sit	sat	sat
sleep	slept	slept
speak	spoke	spoken
spend	spent	spent
stand	stood	stood
take	took	taken
teach	taught	taught
tell	told	told
think	thought	thought
understand	understood	understood
wake	woke	woken
wear	wore	worn
win	won	won
write	wrote	written

Tapescripts

1 Nice to meet you

1.1 Say who you are

SUSIE: Good morning.
OLGA: Morning.
SUSIE: Susie Smith, can I help?
OLGA: Hello, Olga Novotna. Nice to meet you. I'm just looking, thanks. It's very interesting.
SUSIE: Thank you. Is this your first visit to Expo?
OLGA: Yes, it is.
SUSIE: Where are you from?
OLGA: Russia.
SUSIE: Russia. Really? Where do you live?
OLGA: In a small town near Moscow.
SUSIE: How far from Moscow?
OLGA: About 20 kilometres. But the company is in Moscow so I get the train in every day.
SUSIE: Right. And who do you work for?
OLGA: For TechnoSport, a sportswear manufacturer.
SUSIE: OK. Would you like one of our brochures?
OLGA: Yes, thanks.
SUSIE: You're welcome. Here. Take two.
OLGA: OK. Nice meeting you. Maybe see you later.
SUSIE: Yes. Nice to meet you. Thank you. Bye.

1.2 Do it yourself

Exercise 4

SUSIE: So, where are you from, Maria?
MARIA: I'm from Italy.
SUSIE: Really? Are you from Rome?
MARIA: No, I'm not. I'm from Milan. Do you know Milan?
SUSIE: Yes, I went there on holiday last year. It's a lovely place.
MARIA: Yes, it's beautiful. Do you come to Italy often?
SUSIE: No, I don't travel much, maybe two or three times a year for business.
MARIA: Which company do you work for?
SUSIE: I work for Skateline.
MARIA: Skateline? Yes, I know the name. What do you do exactly?
SUSIE: We make inline skates. And you? What do you do?
MARIA: We sell bicycles.

1.3 Sounds good

Exercise 1

MARIA: What do you do exactly?
SUSIE: We make inline skates. And you? What do you do?
MARIA: We sell bicycles.

2 Helping people to learn

2.1 The words you need

Exercise 1

1 I'm part of a consulting company.
2 I work for Språngbrädan.
3 I work in training.

4 I'm responsible for developing democracy.
5 I work closely with three female colleagues.
6 I'm in charge of Eastern Europe.
7 An important part of my job is email contact.
8 I work in the former Soviet Union.

2.2 Telephoning 1: Getting information

Call 1

RECEPTIONIST: CyberProducts. Good morning. How can I help you?
JAKE: Peter Blake.
RECEPTIONIST: Sorry?
JAKE: I want to speak to Peter Blake.
RECEPTIONIST: Connecting you now.
JAKE: OK.
PETER: Peter Blake.
JAKE: Peter. We need a meeting tomorrow to discuss the training course. We have a big problem.
PETER: Sorry, who's calling, please?
JAKE: It's Jake Roberts.
PETER: OK, look Jake, I'm in a meeting right now. Can I call you back in ten minutes?
JAKE: OK.
PETER: Oh ... fine. Thanks for calling.

Call 2

RECEPTIONIST: CyberProducts. Good morning.
JANE: Good morning. Could I speak to Peter Blake, please?
RECEPTIONIST: Certainly. Who's calling, please?
JANE: It's Jane Dawson.
RECEPTIONIST: Just a moment, I'll put you through.
JANE: Thanks.
PETER: Jane. How are you?
JANE: Fine, thanks. And you?
PETER: Fine. How can I help?
JANE: I'm just calling to ask if you want some help with the organisation of the training course next week.
PETER: Thanks, but everything's OK. There's no need for you to do anything.
JANE: Sure?
PETER: Yes, thanks very much.
JANE: OK, great. Have a good training course. Talk to you next week. Bye.
PETER: Yes. Thanks for calling.

3 Have a good weekend

3.1 It's almost the weekend

Arriving at the office on Friday

A: Hi, John.
B: Morning. How are you?
A: Fine, thanks. And you?
B: Not bad. A bit tired.
A: Never mind. It's almost the weekend.

Going for lunch

A: Ready for some lunch?
B: Yes, good idea.
A: Where do you want to eat?
B: Shall we eat out?
A: Yes, it's Friday. The new Italian place?
B: Great. Let's go.

A weekend away

A: Do you have any plans for the weekend?
B: I'm going to visit my brother.
A: Where does he live?
B: In Stratford-upon-Avon.
A: Stratford? It's a lovely place. Have a good time!
B: Thanks. I will!

Going home

A: I'm going. See you next week.
B: OK, see you.
A: Have a good weekend.
B: Thanks. You too. Bye.

3.2 Enjoying your weekend

Exercise 2

Sally

In the summer I usually like to go sailing on the north Norfolk coast, if the wind is good. We try to go every weekend if possible, but it depends on the weather, obviously. If I don't go sailing then I go walking or maybe stay at home.

Hinawi

Cambridge is so beautiful, you can do lots of things here. There are lots of places you can go sightseeing, for example. But I often go to the swimming pool, I like swimming. Sometimes I go to the local sauna. London is quite close as well and we take the train sometimes.

Martina

I usually work during the weekends, because I need extra money, but if I've got some free time I go out, visit my friends, go to the cinema, clubbing, cycling, walking around Cambridge, swimming.

Jochen

One of my hobbies is astronomy. I've got a telescope and I look at stars and planets and things like that. I usually watch from home but sometimes I put the telescopes in the car and go somewhere where you have a really, really dark sky.

4 North and south

4.1 A working day in the north … and in the south of Europe

Anneli

INTERVIEWER: So, what is your job, Anneli?
ANNELI: I'm an assistant administrator with Telia's mobile telephone system.
INTERVIEWER: OK. And how do you organise your working day?
ANNELI: Well, I'm at work at 8, and then first thing, I go through my email. Then we have a short coffee break, have a sandwich, then back to work again.
INTERVIEWER: And when is lunch? I think it's quite early in Scandinavia.
ANNELI: Yeah, for you it's early. I usually eat at 11 for one hour. It's typical in Sweden to bring food to work for lunch. We also have a long coffee break in the afternoon around 2, more drinking coffee, and then go home around 5, something like that.
INTERVIEWER: OK, do you sometimes work late or … ?

ANNELI: No, not very often. My boss often works late. With me, maybe I stay until 8 if I have a big project. That can be stressful sometimes …

Chiara

INTERVIEWER: And Chiara, tell me about a typical working day.
CHIARA: OK, I usually get to work at 9. Then I have a cup of tea, very English, I know. I don't have breakfast at home and so I have a little something to eat here in the office. After that, my emails!
INTERVIEWER: Do you prefer working in the morning or the afternoon?
CHIARA: Oh, I'm more of an afternoon person. I'm not very good in the morning.
INTERVIEWER: OK, so what time do you have lunch?
CHIARA: Around 1 o'clock every day. We have a canteen in our company. So maybe we eat for half an hour and go for a little walk just to have some fresh air.
INTERVIEWER: And what time do you usually finish work?
CHIARA: Around 6 o'clock. And that means I have dinner at around 8, more or less. And I go to bed at around 12, not so late.
INTERVIEWER: Right, and do you ever work weekends?
CHIARA: No, never.
INTERVIEWER: And your boss?
CHIARA: She doesn't like to work at the weekend but sometimes, you know, you have a lot to do. But me, no. Weekends are for me, not work!

4.2 Sounds good

/s/   /z/   /ɪz/
gets   goes   watches

4.3 Sounds good

leaves   writes   relaxes   sells   works   buys   organises
meets   visits   listens   manages   does

5 Health care – public or private?

5.1 Telephoning 2: Could I have your number?

Exercise 1

678586
784367
488598
598889
584989

5.2 Telephoning 2: Can I take a message?

Exercise 2

A: Hello.
B: Could I speak to Mr García?
A: I'm afraid he's in a meeting. Can I take a message?
B: Could you ask him to call me back?
A: Of course. Could I have your name and number?
B: Yes, my name's Fiala. That's F-i-a-l-a.
A: Did you say 'F'?
B: Yes, 'F'. Fiala.
A: OK, so that's F-i-a-l-a.
B: Yes. That's right. And my number is 7877545.
A: 787545.
B: No, 7877545.
A: Double 7 – 545. OK, Mr Fiala, I'll make sure he gets the message.
B: Thank you. Goodbye.

6 Downtown Barcelona

6.1 Shopping

Looking around

A: Hello, can I help you?

B: No, it's OK thanks. I'm just looking.

A: OK. Just ask me if you need some help.

Asking for help

B: Could I try this on, please?

A: Yes, of course. The changing rooms are just there.

B: Thank you.

A: (*A few minutes later*) So, how's that?

B: I'm not sure. It's a bit small. Have you got it in a larger size?

A: No, I'm sorry, we haven't.

B: Oh, I see. I think I'll leave it then.

Asking about the price

B: Excuse me, how much is this, please?

A: It's €47.

B: OK, I'll take it.

A: Fine. You can pay over there.

Asking about payment

A: That's €47, please.

B: Thank you. Can I pay by credit card?

A: Yes, of course. Sign here, please.

B: OK.

A: Here's your card and your receipt is in the bag. Thank you.

B: Thank you. Goodbye.

6.2 A shoppers' paradise

INTERVIEWER: So, where do you live?

MONTSE: I live in downtown Barcelona, or in the city centre, in Eixample, it's called, which is a cultural area with lots of modernist architecture.

INTERVIEWER: Do you like this area?

MONTSE: Yes, I love it. It's very open, the streets are very wide, the flats and the buildings are not very high ... it's a very nice atmosphere.

INTERVIEWER: I think the architecture is nice.

MONTSE: Oh, yes, for example all the Gaudi buildings are around my house. I'm also very near to the Gothic quarter, which is the old centre of Barcelona. It's only ten minutes' walk from my house.

INTERVIEWER: I'm travelling to Barcelona in ten days. Can you recommend something to buy that's typical of the area?

MONTSE: Well, Barcelona is great for shops. I can recommend the hand-made, modernist style gifts. Another thing that is interesting is wine, and Cava.

INTERVIEWER: Is Barcelona good for shopping?

MONTSE: Well, you can find almost anything in Barcelona, it's a shoppers' paradise. But there are two main areas, the Gothic quarter and the Modernist quarter. In the Gothic quarter, you find typical markets where you can buy fresh food, and you have very special shops that are just amazing. In the Modernist area you can find international things – fashion, jewellery, gifts, sophisticated designs. And the prices are good too. It's not so expensive.

INTERVIEWER: Do you have a favourite shop that you like going to?

MONTSE: Let me think ... I like all the shops but maybe my favourite area is the Passeig de Gracia, which is a big avenue, and in that area, this is in the Modernist area, I really like all the different shops there. I'm so lucky. I live in a wonderful city, right next to a great shopping area.

6.3 The words you need

Exercise 1

1 I live in the city centre.

2 I live in quite a small street.

3 I live near the main shopping centre.

4 I live outside Barcelona.

5 Sitges is on the coast.

6 Sitges is about 40 kilometres from Barcelona.

7 Sitges is a small town not far from Barcelona.

8 Barcelona is in the north-east of Spain.

6.4 The words you need

Exercise 2

SAMANTHA: So, let's plan the weekend. Can we go somewhere?

MONTSE: Yes, what about Sitges? It's a really nice place.

SAMANTHA: How far is it from Barcelona?

MONTSE: Not far. By bus it takes about 40 minutes. Or perhaps we could go by train.

SAMANTHA: I'd like to go by bus. Where do we catch it?

MONTSE: The bus station is quite close – it will only take us about five minutes to walk there.

SAMANTHA: Good! And I've got a friend who lives in Vilanova. Is it far from Sitges?

MONTSE: No, it's quite close. We can probably get there by bus. It's a lovely place.

7 Changing workspace

7.1 This is where I work

INTERVIEWER: So, Stein. Tell me about your great new office.

STEIN: Well, there are 7,000 people here. It's a very big building and the idea is to have all employees in one place. But there are no fixed offices or desks for people. Only one person, the Managing Director, has a personal office. All the other people sit where they can and just plug in their portable computer.

INTERVIEWER: What about paper?

STEIN: There's no paper, or very, very little. We want a paperless office with information on a database.

INTERVIEWER: Do employees like this new office system?

STEIN: Oh, yes. I think it's very, very flexible. People can now work when it's good for them to work.

INTERVIEWER: And in this building, are there a lot of things for staff, like a fitness centre or anything they can do after work?

STEIN: Yes, there's a big fitness centre, which people also like a lot. There are also a lot of table games, and a very good restaurant, which is open after people normally go home. The office has everything you want.

INTERVIEWER: Do you like it?

STEIN: Well, yes, I like it a lot. The important thing for me is that I get information very quickly. In the open office, I hear things which I can use in my work. That's good. People talk more, I think.

INTERVIEWER: Is there anything about it that you don't like?

STEIN: OK, maybe there's one little thing I don't like. Sometimes you know, people are people, and sometimes people don't want to be with people, they want to be alone, if they have a bad day, or if they want to think about something. And the problem for me is that with the glass, all the walls in the rooms have glass walls, people can see me if I get angry, which is sometimes not so good.

7.2 Do it yourself

Exercise 2

DAVID: So, is there a car park for employees?

BOB: Yes, there's some space but only for top management.

DAVID: What do other people do?

BOB: Well, there's a railway station nearby so lots of people come by train.

DAVID: I see. What about lunch? Is there a staff restaurant?

BOB: No, but there are a lot of bars and restaurants in the same street.

DAVID: Is there a gym or swimming pool?

BOB: No, there isn't anything like that. But there are two parks across the street and a swimming pool half a kilometre away.

DAVID: Is there somewhere I can get a drink?

BOB: Yes, there are a lot of drinks machines in the building. Let's get something.

7.3 Sounds good

Exercise 1

1 There is a big problem.
2 There is a big fitness centre.
3 There are a lot of small cafés.

7.4 Sounds good

Exercise 2

1 Telenor is a big company.
2 It's a very big building.
3 I think it's very, very flexible.
4 There's a big fitness centre, which is very good.
5 Yes, I like it a lot.

8 The A team

8.1 Meeting a visitor at the airport

SHIRLEY: Hi, Koji. It's good to see you again. How are you?

KOJI: Hello! I'm fine, thanks. What about you?

SHIRLEY: Not too bad. A little tired. Too much work, you know.

KOJI: I know the problem.

SHIRLEY: Did you have a good trip?

KOJI: Not too bad. A little delay when I left but nothing serious.

SHIRLEY: Good. Here, can I help you with your luggage?

KOJI: Thank you. Could you take this?

SHIRLEY: Of course. No problem. Now follow me. The car's in the car park.

KOJI: OK. Wow, it's so warm here! It's beautiful.

SHIRLEY: Yeah, it's been great recently. How's the weather back home?

KOJI: Really cold right now. So this is nice!

SHIRLEY: Good. Well, welcome to the sun! This is it. Let me put your bags in the back and we can …

9 I love Chicago

9.1 Getting around

Buying a ticket

A: Hi. Three tickets for the Wendella Lake tour, please. Two adults and one child.

B: That's $22.50, please.

A: Thanks. What time does the next ferry leave, please?

B: At 3 o'clock, in 25 minutes.

A: OK. Thanks.

Taking the train

A: Excuse me. Does this go to O'Hare Airport?

B: No. You need to take the blue line.

A: OK, so where do I go?

B: Go to Lake Street and transfer to the blue line and then take it to the end of the line.

A: Great. Thanks for your help.

Catching a bus

A: Excuse me. Can I get a bus to the Magnificent Mile from here?

B: Yes, you want a number 151 or a 147. Or you can take a cab or walk.

A: When's the next bus?

B: Ten minutes. But they're not always on time.

A: Thanks.

Getting a cab

A: How much is that?

B: That's $10.20.

A: Here you are, $12.00. Keep the change.

B: Thank you.

A: Could I have a receipt?

B: Sure. Here you go. Have a good day.

9.2 It's my kind of town

INTERVIEWER: So, where do you live, in Chicago or just outside?

ELLEN: I live in the centre of the city in an area called the Magnificent Mile, or the Gold Coast, which is the centre of all restaurants, bars and shopping.

INTERVIEWER: And do you like living in Chicago?

ELLEN: Like it? I love it. It's beautiful, really beautiful. It's a nice place to live, very clean and organised. Maybe the thing I like most about it is the number of ethnic restaurants. I think you can eat food from any country in the world here.

INTERVIEWER: What's your favourite restaurant then?

ELLEN: My new thing is Middle Eastern so I go to Persian, Turkish and Iraqi restaurants, or my favourite, yes, of course, is a fantastic Lebanese restaurant – Lebanese food is my favourite – where for five bucks you get an amazing meal and the best lentil soup in the world!

INTERVIEWER: What is there to see and do?

ELLEN: Well, we are famous for the first skyscraper in the country. I think it went up in 1885. And we have the Sears Tower, the tallest building in North America, OK not the world, but tourists typically do that.

INTERVIEWER: Chicago is famous for music too?

ELLEN: Sure, Chicago *is* music. Louis Armstrong was big here and you can listen to lots of blues and jazz. But we have a lot of things here like a jazz festival, a film festival, and a baseball team, the Chicago Cubs – and do you know the Taste of Chicago?

INTERVIEWER: No, what's that?

ELLEN: It's a big eating day – like a very big barbecue in the park. Three million people come and visit for the day in summer and eat, eat, eat – 237,000 pieces of pizza and 120,000 turkey legs. It's really amazing and the quality is excellent. You know, fast food is part of the culture. The first McDonald's was in 1955 in Chicago.

INTERVIEWER: Is there anything you don't like? People have this idea that it's quite dangerous, is that true?

ELLEN: Well, it's famous for Al Capone, of course. But I know New York City and I can say I feel safe here in Chicago. No, I can maybe say it's expensive but that's all. I don't want to live anywhere else. Chicago is my home and it's great!

10 Eating around the world

10.1 Favourite food

INTERVIEWER: Ablaziz, you're from France. Can I ask you first, what do you think about English food?

ABLAZIZ: Well, English food for me can be very, very good, perhaps a little heavy but very good. I think the idea of bad English food is a cliché now. The food is better than in the past.

INTERVIEWER: But you think English food is heavier than French food?

ABLAZIZ: Yes, it is heavier than French food. French food is lighter. In England I think you often have a big piece of something like meat, and often fatty food, which is maybe too heavy.

INTERVIEWER: What about price? Is English food more expensive?

ABLAZIZ: I think, generally, the price is similar. But in London, it's interesting, it's more expensive than you find in Paris, much more expensive.

INTERVIEWER: Which food do you like the most?

ABLAZIZ: Italian food, because it's very simple. There's a lot of pasta, a lot of starters with vegetables, a lot of sauces so I think it's quite light, not heavy. But I have to say, if I have a birthday, I eat foie gras, a typical French dish.

INTERVIEWER: I know you travel to the Middle East sometimes. How is the food there?

ABLAZIZ: In Jordan and in Israel, it's like Mediterranean food, like Greek food, very light with lots of small dishes and different choices. Nice.

INTERVIEWER: Do you think the food there is better than in Europe?

ABLAZIZ: No, I can't say that it's better. It's different. French food and Italian food is the food I prefer but I can't say which is the best.

INTERVIEWER: Do you like spicy food?

ABLAZIZ: Yes, Indian, for example. Indian is spicier than French food generally. And yes, I like it.

INTERVIEWER: Finally, just a question about food and business. People say that eating is an important part of business. Do you agree?

ABLAZIZ: Yes, you meet a lot of people in business around lunch or dinner. Restaurants are the best place to discuss business, with good food and a good atmosphere. So it's good because, for me, eating good food is one of the most important things in life.

10.2 Do it yourself

Exercise 2

1 Fresh fruit is healthier than chocolate.
2 Salmon is cheaper than Russian caviar.
3 Champagne is more expensive than Cava.
4 A sandwich is quicker to eat than a meal in a restaurant.
5 Indian food is spicier than English food.

10.3 Sounds good

Exercise 1

The Pentium 3 processor is cheaper than the Pentium 4.
Bordeaux wines are amongst the most famous wines in the world.

10.4 Sounds good

Exercise 2

1 Polite? We're politer than the rest.
2 Fast? We're faster than the rest.
3 Cheap? We're less expensive than the rest.
4 Big? We're the biggest in the world.
5 Good? We're the best in the world.

12 Do you salsa?

12.1 I've got news for you

Responding to good news

A: Hi. Good weekend?
B: Yes, very. I have some news. My wife's pregnant.
A: Wonderful. Congratulations!
B: Thanks. We're very happy.
A: Oh, good. We must celebrate.

Responding to interesting news

A: Hey, Peter. I've got an email from China.
B: Really?
A: Yes, it's a new customer, I think. They want information about our products.
B: Great. Please tell me if you hear any more from them.
A: Of course I will.

Responding to bad news

A: So you leave for the US tonight?
B: Don't ask! My trip's cancelled!
A: Why's that?
B: Because I have to stay here for a meeting with my boss.
A: Oh, well, never mind. Now you can come to Helen's party tonight.

Responding to surprising news

A: See you tomorrow.
B: Yeah, see you. What are you doing tonight?
A: I'm not sure yet. I might go jogging.
B: You're joking! I don't believe it. You hate sport.
A: Yes, but I need the exercise.

12.2 I hate watching TV

Ben

INTERVIEWER: So Ben, do you do any sport?

BEN: At the weekend, I do a lot of sport. I play tennis and squash, the usual things. But I also do a lot of motorcycle racing – I have a 1954 Triumph 650 cc. I usually race with around 20 other bikes at about eight to ten meetings a year. It's a lot of work to maintain the bike but it's very exciting. I never win, but that's not important. I just like to meet people who have the same interest.

Alison

INTERVIEWER: And Alison, are you a sporty person?

ALISON: Yes, I am. I like flying and I also sometimes go scuba diving. For the flying, I go around six times a year – and for scuba diving, maybe around eight times. The only problem is that both sports are quite expensive. Flying costs about £100 per hour and scuba diving about the same. And another thing with scuba diving, the sea around the UK is really cold!

INTERVIEWER: Do you like the danger of these sports?

ALISON: Flying and scuba diving are not dangerous. No, I like flying because I like being alone in the air and so I can relax. And diving, I like it because it's good exercise.

Roisin

INTERVIEWER: Roisin, how about you? Do you do much sport?

ROISIN: Not really sport. I go dancing, salsa dancing, once a week – anything from two to four hours, which is a whole evening. And dancing is very energetic and great fun. I also try to go swimming once or twice a week. It's good to relax after work, which is very stressful sometimes.

INTERVIEWER: Do you ever watch sport on TV?

ROISIN: No, never! People watch too much television. It's better to go out and do something! I hate sport on TV, especially football!

13 Chanel

13.1 Gabrielle (Coco) Chanel – inventor of the fashion industry

INTERVIEWER: OK, Julie. Can you tell me a little bit about Coco Chanel? And first, the name. Why Coco?

JULIE: That's easy. The name Coco comes from a song she always sang, Cocorico, which became Coco.

INTERVIEWER: Tell us about her life.

JULIE: Well, she was born in France, in the Loire region, in 1883. The first important date is 1910 when she opened her first clothes shop, I think the name was Chanel Modes, Chanel Fashion in English.

INTERVIEWER: When did she launch the famous Chanel Number 5?

JULIE: Chanel Number 5? That was much later, in 1921. And I need to tell you about the name, why Chanel Number 5. It's very simple. They tested many perfumes, they didn't like the first four but number five was fantastic. And so, number five tested was the perfume they chose to sell, and so got the name Chanel Number 5.

INTERVIEWER: I see. And after that, what did she do?

JULIE: Well, she did a lot of things. One important thing, in 1924, she worked with Pierre and Paul Wertheimer to create Société des Parfums Chanel, which you can still find today. But it wasn't always a happy life.

INTERVIEWER: Why not?

JULIE: Well, she had some problems during the Second World War, she had some connections, some communication, with the Nazis and so she left France after the war and moved to Switzerland in 1946. She only returned to Paris in 1954. It was a long time before she had a good position again. In fact, Yves Saint Laurent held a fashion show for her in 1967 and this was the start of her comeback. It was very important for her.

INTERVIEWER: I know that she died in 1971. But you still see Chanel's influence today, especially with modern businesswomen.

JULIE: Oh, yes. Coco Chanel changed women's lives. She was the first designer to use the two-piece suit for women, to use men's clothes for women. And this was a big, big change at that time. And, I think it's very important to women today, especially in business. So, I think, wherever you go, you can still see the fashion of Coco Chanel.

13.2 Do it yourself

Exercise 4

GENEVIEVE: Afternoon, Peter. You look tired! What did you do last night?

PETER: Hi, I went to a restaurant for an early dinner and then to the cinema.

GENEVIEVE: What did you see?

PETER: A Russian film. It was about a family in Moscow. I don't remember the title.

GENEVIEVE: Was it good?

PETER: No, it wasn't. I didn't understand it really.

13.3 Sounds good

Exercise 1

/ɪd/	/t/	/d/
wanted	walked	played

13.4 Sounds good

Exercise 2

liked decreased decided looked wanted increased
enjoyed talked received listened walked visited

13.5 Sounds good

Exercise 3

bring – brought   buy – bought   read – read   say – said
see – saw   speak – spoke   take – took   tell – told
think – thought

14 Médecins Sans Frontières

14.1 Visiting an organisation

At reception

KEIKO: Good morning. My name's Keiko Sumi. I've got an appointment with Patrick Hart at 10 o'clock.

RECEPTIONIST: Just a moment, Ms Sumi. I'll tell him you're here. Could you sign the visitors' book?

KEIKO: Of course.

RECEPTIONIST: Right. Mr Hart will be with you in a moment.

KEIKO: Thank you.

RECEPTIONIST: And could you put on this security badge, please?

14.2 Visiting an organisation

At the office

PATRICK: Hello, Patrick Hart. Nice to meet you.

KEIKO: Hello, Keiko Sumi. Nice to meet you.

PATRICK: Please follow me. We can go to my office.

KEIKO: Great.

PATRICK: And is this your first trip to London?

KEIKO: No, I've been here twice before.

PATRICK: So, here we are. Please take a seat.

KEIKO: Thank you.

PATRICK: Can I get you a drink? Tea, coffee …

KEIKO: Coffee would be great.

PATRICK: No problem.

KEIKO: So, how many people work here?
PATRICK: 250 people work in this building. It's our headquarters.
KEIKO: I see.

15 Trekking in Nepal

15.1 Getting there

Checking in
A: Can I check in here for Vienna?
B: Yes. Can I see your passport and ticket, please?
A: Of course.
B: Would you prefer a window or an aisle seat?
A: An aisle seat, please.
B: Boarding is at 17.30 at gate 45.

Getting information at the gate
A: Excuse me, do you have any information about the Amsterdam flight?
B: Yes, the flight is delayed by 45 minutes.
A: OK, so when is boarding?
B: Boarding is now at 18.30. I'm very sorry for the delay.

On the plane
A: Excuse me, could you put your bag in the overhead locker?
B: They're full. There's no room.
A: Can you put it under your seat?
B: OK, I'll do that.
A: Thank you.

Arriving without luggage
A: Hello, my suitcase didn't arrive.
B: Right, I need some information from you.
A: OK, this is my flight information and a local address.
B: Thank you. You're very organised.
A: Yes, this isn't the first time!

15.2 Walking at 5,000 metres
INTERVIEWER: So, Jürgen. Tell me about your best holiday.
JÜRGEN: Well, it was definitely my trekking holiday in Nepal.
INTERVIEWER: OK. When did you go?
JÜRGEN: I went to Nepal about 10 years ago on a trekking tour, to do some walking in the mountains.
INTERVIEWER: How long did you go for?
JÜRGEN: The trekking tour was about 25 days from Kathmandu to very close to the Everest base camp.
INTERVIEWER: 25 days! That's a long time. How far did you walk every day?
JÜRGEN: That's quite difficult. Not really far, I think. Perhaps, 18 kilometres. But you have to climb up and down a lot every day.
INTERVIEWER: So, it was very hard trekking?
JÜRGEN: Yeah, very hard trekking. Sometimes, you have problems walking at only five thousand metres where the air is very thin, and you have a lot of problems with not enough oxygen.
INTERVIEWER: What kind of equipment did you take with you?
JÜRGEN: Not much. Only a rucksack, a sleeping bag and some warm clothing and that's all. There are a lot of lodges and so equipment is not a problem. But you need a good sleeping bag to keep out the cold, believe me.
INTERVIEWER: And how was the food?
JÜRGEN: Good. There was a lot of rice and in the higher mountains a lot of potatoes and only a few vegetables, normally no beef, no meat. But it was good, very good.

INTERVIEWER: How many people were you walking with?
JÜRGEN: I was travelling only with my wife so there were just two of us. And we carried all our things by ourselves, so no porters. We saw some people at night in the lodges but during the day we walked alone.
INTERVIEWER: What was the best thing about the trip?
JÜRGEN: The walking and the exercise. I hate holidays where you sit and sunbathe. I like to be out in the countryside, and in Nepal, at four or five thousand metres, it's perfect. The air is very clean, it's very quiet, it's just a beautiful place. You must go!

Revision 1

R1.1 Pronunciation
Exercise 1
1 We have a message for you.
2 It's about our company.
3 It's a great place to work.
4 We need another 50 people.
5 So come and join us.

R1.2 Pronunciation
Exercise 2
played   needed   liked   decreased   decided   looked   enjoyed   listened   walked   visited

16 Project Stockholm

16.1 What project are you working on at the moment?
INTERVIEWER: So, what is your name and what do you do?
RIGGERT: My name is Riggert Andersson and I'm a project manager working for the Swedish Railroad Authority. I have about 200 people working in the projects that I am managing.
INTERVIEWER: What project are you working on at the moment?
RIGGERT: At the moment, we have two big projects and with both projects the idea is to have more railroad capacity into Stockholm and through Stockholm. My project is a new bridge called Årstabron, more or less in the city centre.
INTERVIEWER: OK, and who designed the bridge?
RIGGERT: Sir Norman Foster designed it. He won an international competition and we are very happy with it.
INTERVIEWER: What is so good about his design?
RIGGERT: It's perfect for the environment. This is a very sensitive part of Stockholm and there is already a bridge in that area. But the new bridge goes with both very well.
INTERVIEWER: So you have to be very sensitive to those kinds of environmental issues?
RIGGERT: Yes, absolutely. When you build anything in Sweden, it's very important to think about the environment.
INTERVIEWER: What exactly are you working on at the moment, which part of the bridge?
RIGGERT: We are working on the foundations and the pillars and want to start with the top part of the bridge soon.
INTERVIEWER: Are you enjoying it?

RIGGERT: Very much indeed, it's a very interesting job. It has everything; it's not only a technical job, it's also a job with a lot of other things. I work a lot with local people. I'm talking and listening all the time to people living close to the railroad, giving information and so on. I like that part of the job.

INTERVIEWER: And are you speaking a lot of English in the project at the moment?

RIGGERT: Not very much at the moment. We have some groups coming to visit the project from other countries and then we use English as the main language. It's increasing and when we get further into the project there will be more.

16.2 Do it yourself

Exercise 3

HELGE: Hi, Lars. What are you working on at the moment?

LARS: I'm so busy. We're reorganising the department right now and it's a lot of work.

HELGE: Really? Where's Anita?

LARS: Anita isn't working this week. She's on holiday. What about you? Are you busy?

HELGE: Very busy. I'm working on a new marketing project.

LARS: Really, but you always say you don't like marketing!

HELGE: Yeah, but actually, this project is quite interesting. We're developing a new sun cream.

LARS: Does the market need another sun cream?

HELGE: Oh, yes. More and more people are travelling abroad these days.

LARS: Lucky people. I never go on holiday – I don't have the time.

16.3 Sounds good

Exercise 1

1 One, two, three.
2 I'm working on a special project.
3 Are you staying in a hotel near here?

16.4 Sounds good

Exercise 2

A: Are you working from home next week?
B: Yes, I'm working from home to the end of the month.
A: Are you busy?
B: Yes, but I'm enjoying the work.

18 Slow food

18.1 Restaurant talk

At the restaurant

A: Good evening. I have a reservation. My name's Brillakis.
B: Yes, the table by the window. Can I take your coats?
A: Thank you.
C: Thanks.
B: So, the menu and the wine list. Would you like a drink before you order?

Before the meal

B: Are you ready to order?
C: Yes. We'll both have the pâté as a starter, please. What's John Dory?
B: John Dory is a kind of white sea fish.
C: Then I'll have the John Dory.
A: The salmon, please.
B: Right. And to drink?
A: We'll have a bottle of the house white.

During the meal

B: Is everything all right?
C: Yes, thanks. Oh, can I have some more bread, please?
B: Sure. And would you like some more wine?
A: No, thanks. Actually, could we have a bottle of sparkling mineral water?

After the meal

B: So, did you enjoy your meal?
C: Yes, thank you. It was very nice.
B: Good. And would you like anything else? More coffee?
C: No, thank you. Could we have the bill, please?
B: Of course.

18.2 A great place to eat

INTERVIEWER: So, what is Slow Food?

WENDY: Well, the Slow Food idea began in 1986. In that year, McDonald's opened a fast food restaurant in a very historic piazza in Rome. This was terrible. So, many people wanted to create an organisation to promote traditional Italian food and Italian food culture.

INTERVIEWER: But the movement is now international?

WENDY: Yes, it is. The movement became international in 1989. There was a congress in Paris on 14th July, Bastille Day and now the organisation has 65,000 members in 45 countries around the world.

INTERVIEWER: And why do so many people like the idea of Slow Food?

WENDY: Many people don't like fast food or mass-produced food because it needs cheap meat, which means a lot of intensive, very industrial farming. And intensive farming is bad for animals, bad for the taste of meat, and may be bad for us. Think about the problems with meat in England over the last few years.

INTERVIEWER: OK, and what for you is a good restaurant?

WENDY: I think the most important thing is that the ingredients are local, you know where possible. We like a restaurant to promote local food. We also love it when a menu is simple. We think you can have some great flavours by making the dishes as simple as possible.

INTERVIEWER: Do you have a favourite restaurant?

WENDY: Yes, in London there's a restaurant called St John with a chef called Fergus Henderson. He's a very instinctive cook. He gets his products from local producers he knows. And, with him, you can have a very basic dish and it will taste fantastic because it is so simple and the quality of the products is so great. So I think that's probably one of my favourites.

INTERVIEWER: Are there any other reasons that you like this restaurant?

WENDY: I think it's very friendly, all of the staff know about food and about wine, they are all very well trained. And that's another important thing for Slow Food. We believe fast food means lower quality of food and lower quality of service. Slow means good – good food and good service.

19 Living in Hong Kong

19.1 Chinese culture

INTERVIEWER: Did you enjoy your time in Hong Kong?

JOHN: Yeah, it was a fantastic time. It's a very dynamic place.

INTERVIEWER: In business, when you meet people for the first time, can you use a first name quickly?

JOHN: Not really, it depends. The thing to say is that there are two Hong Kongs, a traditional Hong Kong with the older people and a young western Hong Kong. Young people move to first names quickly. With a traditional person, you have to use the surname to start with.

INTERVIEWER: And is it important to be on time in business?

JOHN: Yes, very important. Hong Kong is a very fast-moving place, people are always in a hurry and so yes, you really have to be on time if you want to do business.

INTERVIEWER: I have a friend who says it's typical to ask about salary, is that true?

JOHN: Yes, it's true, you can ask about salary. People are very open about money questions generally, and salary is a money question. So, don't be surprised if people ask you about that.

INTERVIEWER: And should you dress formally?

JOHN: Yes, formally to start with. Hong Kong is a very fashionable place, so you should dress well. You don't have to wear designer labels, but you should be smart.

INTERVIEWER: About general life, I think family is very important in Hong Kong culture?

JOHN: Yes, traditionally. In the past, families lived together – children, parents and grandparents. And there was a strong sense of family. Now, modern houses and flats are so small, families can't live together now, so things are changing.

INTERVIEWER: And are there any rules about tipping in taxis and restaurants, things like that?

JOHN: In Hong Kong tipping is very important. In restaurants you should tip, say ten per cent or 15 per cent, or more if you're very happy with the service.

INTERVIEWER: And finally, is there anything I should be careful about?

JOHN: Well, if you're in a train in the underground, and you want to get out, when the door opens, people often just push on before you can get out. It makes some tourists very angry. But the people are not rude, they simply want to do business quickly. You know, time is money in Hong Kong.

19.2 Do it yourself

Exercise 3

JAMES: Do you have to start work at the same time every day?

COLLEAGUE: No. You can choose any time between 7.30 and 9.30.

JAMES: Do you have to work 40 hours every week?

COLLEAGUE: Yes, you have to work the hours in your contract.

JAMES: Do you have to wear a tie at work?

COLLEAGUE: You don't have to unless you are meeting a customer.

JAMES: Should I buy my boss a present? It's her birthday tomorrow.

COLLEAGUE: Yes, you should, but just something simple and not too expensive.

JAMES: Should I inform Peter about the computer problem?

COLLEAGUE: Yes, I think you should. He wants to know about any IT questions.

JAMES: Should I send him an email to confirm the meeting?

COLLEAGUE: No, you don't have to. I've already told him the time and place.

19.3 Sounds good

Exercise 1

China   Chinese

19.4 Sounds good

Exercise 2

1 Yeah, it was a fantastic time ...
2 It's a very dynamic place.
3 With a traditional person ...
4 People are very open about money ...
5 Hong Kong is a very fashionable place ...
6 I think family is very important ...
7 ... modern houses and flats ...
8 ... ten or 15 per cent ...

20 Online

20.1 Telephoning 3: Arranging meetings

Philippe

PHILIPPE: Jim, is it possible to have a meeting next week? I'd like to discuss some technical problems with our computer network.

JIM: Sure, Philippe, no problem. When are you free?

PHILIPPE: What about next Friday at two o'clock, after lunch?

JIM: Fine. Can you send me an email to confirm that?

PHILIPPE: OK. See you next week. Bye.

Frank

FRANK: Jim, it's Frank. I'm calling to fix a meeting next week to discuss the Bolivia project. When are you free?

JIM: What about Monday at 12 o'clock?

FRANK: I'm sorry, I can't. I have another meeting. What about 1 o'clock?

JIM: OK, 1 on Monday.

FRANK: Thanks, Jim. Bye.

Petra

PETRA: Jim, it's Petra. How are you?

JIM: I'm fine. How are you?

PETRA: Fine. I'm calling because I'm in town next week. Are you free at all?

JIM: Sure. When?

PETRA: For me, Tuesday would be best ... at ten o'clock?

JIM: Just a moment ... yes, that's fine. See you on Tuesday at 10.

PETRA: Great. And I have those pictures from the conference for you.

JIM: Really? Great. See you next week, Petra. Take care. Bye.

21 Beirut Intercontinental

21.1 Enjoy your stay

Checking in

A: Hello, my name's Sanchez, I have a reservation.

B: Good evening. Yes, Mr Sanchez, a single room, for two nights. Could you complete this form, please?

A: Of course.

B: Thank you. So, it's room 414, on the fourth floor. Do you need any help with your bags?

A: No, thanks. I can manage.

A morning call

A: Hello, can I have breakfast in my room, please? At 7 o'clock?

B: Certainly, sir.

A: So I'd like a wake-up call at 6.30. Can you do that?

B: That's fine. So, morning call at 6.30, breakfast at 7 o'clock.

A problem

A: Good morning. There's a problem with the shower. There's no hot water. Can you send someone to look at it?

B: Of course, I'll send someone immediately. What's your room number?

A: 414.

B: Fine. Someone will be with you in a moment.

Leaving

A: Morning, can I check out, please? Room 414.

B: Right, Mr Sanchez. Anything from the minibar last night?

A: No, nothing.

B: OK, here's your bill. Sign here, please. Have a good trip home.

21.2 It's a great place to stay

BOB: So, where is my favourite hotel? It's difficult but I think my favourite, favourite hotel is Le Vendôme Intercontinental in Beirut. It's only a four-star hotel because it doesn't have a swimming pool but for me it's perfect. It's small – it only has about 70 rooms so it's very cosy. The staff are very friendly, they always remember my name, even the chambermaids. I like good food, and Le Vendôme has a first-class French restaurant. I love French food, you know! And ... oh yes, just outside the door there is a very, very nice fountain which I like, in the Spanish style. I stay there quite a lot and for me it's like going home to see friends. They meet you at the airport, take you straight to your room, there are no forms to fill in ... you feel very, very comfortable. And one more thing, on the roof there is a really famous bar called Sidney's where they serve the breakfasts in the morning. It has a beautiful view over the Mediterranean with the fishing boats ... mmm, I think I can smell the coffee and the sea ...

22 Working for Rolls Royce

22.1 Work is like a second home

INTERVIEWER: So, Isabelle, how many people work for Rolls Royce?

ISABELLE: Well, Rolls Royce Group is a big company but our office in France is a small representative office with only four people: two directors, one engineer and myself.

INTERVIEWER: So what is a typical day? How much time do you spend on the telephone and with email?

ISABELLE: Well, first of all I make myself a big cup of coffee. That is very important. Then, the telephone. OK, it's not too bad but I have a lot of emails to write and read, so this takes maybe around 75 to 80% of my time.

INTERVIEWER: What about meetings? Do you go to many meetings?

ISABELLE: No, I don't, no. In France, a lot of people spend too much time in meetings, but I'm lucky. I have to go to a few, maybe two a week, but not too many.

INTERVIEWER: And how many hours per week do you work?

ISABELLE: Well, as you know, in France we have a 35-hour working week now, so I start work at nine, have one hour for lunch and finish at five-fifteen. Of course, the directors work a lot more, sometimes at weekends. But for me, the 35-hour working week is good. I even leave at four-thirty on Fridays sometimes.

INTERVIEWER: What about benefits and holidays?

ISABELLE: Well, that one is easy, no benefits at all. I mean, no mobile phone, or company car, no, not for me. It's a pity! Holidays? Well, it's now six weeks and I normally take three weeks in August, which is typical in France.

INTERVIEWER: And, one final question, do you like your job?

ISABELLE: I do like my job, yes, because ... well, I like working for a British company. I speak and work in English all day and that's really very nice for me, I like that. I also feel like a member of the team rather than just a secretary. And, generally, working here, it's like a second home. It's a real pleasure to come here every day.

22.2 Sounds good

Exercise 1

Numbers

twenty-five

a hundred *or* one hundred

a hundred and one *or* one hundred and one

a thousand *or* one thousand

two thousand and one

ten thousand five hundred and fifty

five hundred thousand

a million *or* one million

a billion *or* one billion

Prices

fifty p

four pounds ninety-nine p *or* four pounds ninety-nine

two hundred and fifty pounds

a hundred and fifty thousand euros *or* one hundred and fifty thousand euros

a hundred and fifty million pounds *or* one hundred and fifty million pounds

ninety-nine cents

four dollars ninety-five cents *or* four dollars ninety-five

two thousand five hundred dollars

two point five million dollars *or* two and a half million dollars

23 Start up

23.1 Helping visitors

1

A: Excuse me, I think I'm lost. Can you tell me where Room 101, is?

B: I can show you.

A: Really? That's very kind of you.

B: No problem. Follow me.

2

A: Your bill.
B: Thank you. Oh no. Caroline?
C: What is it?
B: I don't have any money. I'm really sorry.
C: Do you want to borrow some money?
B: Can I? Twenty euros? I'll pay you back tomorrow.
C: No problem. Here you are.
B: Thanks.

3

A: Excuse me. I need to send an email. Can I plug in my computer?
B: Would you like to use a computer here?
A: Yes, thanks.
B: The computer in the corner is free.
A: Thank you for your help.

4

A: Sandra, could you recommend a restaurant for me tonight?
B: Sure. There's an excellent Chinese place I know.
A: Great. Where is it?
B: I can show you on the map, if you want.
A: Yes, thanks.

24 I buy money

24.1 Money talk

Asking a colleague for money

A: Clare, I haven't got much cash on me.
B: Do you want to borrow some money?
A: Could you lend me ten pounds until tomorrow?
B: No problem.
A: Cheers. That's very nice of you.

Getting money out

A: Shall we find a restaurant?
B: Yes, but I need to get some money out first.
A: OK, I'll wait here.
B: Is there a cash point nearby?
A: Yes, there's a bank just across the road, over there.

Changing money

A: Hello, I'd like to change some euros into Swiss francs.
B: How much do you want to change?
A: What's the commission?
B: There's no commission if you change more than 200 euros.
A: OK, then I'll change 300, thanks.

Getting change

A: Excuse me, do you have any change?
B: What do you need?
A: I need some coins for the coffee machine.
B: Just a second, yes, here you are.
A: Thanks very much.

24.2 Hey, big spender

1

INTERVIEWER: Anne, what do you spend your money on?
ANNE: I like shopping for clothes. That's my usual Saturday morning activity. But I don't spend a lot. I look for reasonable prices.
INTERVIEWER: OK, and anything else?
ANNE: Not really. I save money every year so that I can have a good holiday. This year it's China. Oh, and one final thing, of course, about money. I have five cats and so I spend a lot of money on cat food.

2

INTERVIEWER: What kind of things do you spend money on?
TASHI: Well, I have an unusual hobby, I'm very interested in old coins. You could say I buy money. And I really like unusual ones so I have some from China, Tibet and Bhutan, for example, and some interesting ones from Greece too. I ask people I meet about coins and if I see something very unusual on the street I buy it, and when I travel I also try and get some for my collection.
INTERVIEWER: Do you like spending money?
TASHI: Actually no, I don't, but I do spend it! I think I should be saving but I keep spending. I don't know where I spend it, it just goes. If I see some coins I buy them and if I see some nice clothes I buy them, I mean without thinking about whether I have the money or not!

3

INTERVIEWER: So, Sam, what do you spend your money on at the weekend?
SAM: Everything. I'm terrible. I'm really bad with money. My purse is always empty! But every Saturday morning I always buy Belgian chocolate for my friends and then we have a coffee together in the city. I'm very generous with chocolate!
INTERVIEWER: Sounds nice. Do you buy anything special?
SAM: Shoes! I love shoes. I buy new shoes almost every month.
INTERVIEWER: Every month? What does your husband say?
SAM: Oh, he's a dangerous shopper too!

25 Driving to Romania

25.1 A job everyone wants to do

INTERVIEWER: So, Anthony, tell me a little about your organisation and what you do.
ANTHONY: I work for a local hospital. And in the Selsey Romania Orphans Appeal, I'm the chairman, and main coordinator, so everything, really. I started the Selsey Romania Orphans Appeal in 1991, I think it was.
INTERVIEWER: And why did you start the charity?
ANTHONY: I saw a lot of television programmes about Romanian children's homes with babies in a terrible, terrible situation, and I had to help. So we organised people to go out there, and now we have around 28 people all in all who support our work, and I think we make a difference to the quality of life for these children.
INTERVIEWER: What do you do out in Romania?
ANTHONY: Well, our first and main objective was to make the children's homes a better place to live. When we arrived, they were terrible: no fresh water, no modern toilet system, no clean kitchens, you can't imagine. There was so much to do to make things like a normal place to live.
INTERVIEWER: You've done a lot of work already. Is there still a lot to do in the future?
ANTHONY: Oh, yes. Absolutely. Eight of us, I think, no nine, are travelling there later this year in October to start a new project.
INTERVIEWER: And how are you getting there?
ANTHONY: Well, we're not flying, we're driving, believe it or

not! We have an old bus and we normally hire a van to take out all the usual things like clothes and toys and even building materials.

INTERVIEWER: How long are you staying?

ANTHONY: We're staying for two weeks. Two weeks is the normal period. And this time we want to install new washing machines and also take some medical equipment. Then the big, big project next year is to build a hospital.

INTERVIEWER: Wow, this sounds like a big job. Is it hard work?

ANTHONY: Not at all. We go because we want to go, because we want to help. No one gets any money or salary in the charity, not one pound, dollar or euro. We're all volunteers. This is one job that everyone is very, very happy to do.

INTERVIEWER: Where do you get the finance for your projects?

ANTHONY: People give us money. We get nothing from the government – just ordinary people, people want to help too and the best way they can do that is to give money to us so that we can give the help directly to the children.

INTERVIEWER: Thanks, Anthony. Good luck with all your projects.

ANTHONY: Thank you very much.

25.2 Do it yourself

Exercise 2

ANTHONY: Anna, it's Anthony. I just wanted to discuss the hospital schedule and check you agree with everything.

ANNA: Sure. Go ahead.

ANTHONY: OK, we're not meeting the architects in October. We're seeing them in November instead.

ANNA: Right. So when are you going to Bucharest for the meeting with the government officials?

ANTHONY: On 18th December. And just before that, on December 14th, we're running a seminar to inform everyone in SROA about the project. Are you still coming to England next year?

ANNA: Yes, in January.

ANTHONY: Good. Well, we're having a tour of my local hospital at the end of January to meet some doctors who are part of the project. I think that's everything.

ANNA: Good. See you soon.

25.3 Sounds good

Exercise 1

1 When are you going to Romania?
2 When are you going to Romania?

25.4 Sounds good

Exercise 2

A: What are you doing next week?
B: I'm going to Poland.
A: Poland? What are you doing there?
B: I'm visiting a friend.
A: How long are you staying?
B: Just for a few days.
A: When are you coming back?
B: Next Friday.
A: Are you doing anything at the weekend?
B: Yes, I'm going camping.

26 Out of order

26.1 Telephoning 4: Solving problems by phone

Call 1

MARIA: Hi, Annie. It's Maria. I'm sorry but I'm having a problem with my computer.

ANNIE: What sort of problem?

MARIA: It keeps crashing for no reason. Could you get someone to check it?

ANNIE: Don't worry. I'll ask an engineer to check. Is that OK?

MARIA: Wonderful. Thank you. Bye.

Call 2

JULIE: Hello, Annie. It's Julie from Excom. I'm sorry but I didn't get the minutes from our last meeting.

ANNIE: Really? I sent them last week in an attachment.

JULIE: Well, I don't think they arrived. Could you send them again?

ANNIE: Sure. I'm really sorry about that. I'll do it now. Call me back in 30 minutes if you still haven't got it.

JULIE: That's great.

Call 3

PETER: Hi, Annie. It's Peter. I can't remember the time of our meeting next week.

ANNIE: Tuesday at 10 o'clock.

PETER: That's fine. Could you contact Jan? I forgot to tell him about it.

ANNIE: Of course. I'll call him straightaway. Do you want me to call back after I speak to him?

PETER: No, only call back if you don't reach him.

27 Teaching T'ai Chi

27.1 Inviting

Inviting someone

SUE: Vasili, I'd like to invite you to lunch tomorrow after our meeting.

VASILI: Oh, thank you very much.

SUE: There's a Mexican restaurant nearby. Is that OK for you?

VASILI: That sounds good.

SUE: Good. I'll reserve a table.

Saying 'maybe' to an invitation

SUE: We're having a little party at the weekend. Can you and Jitka come?

BERNDT: That sounds nice. Thank you. But I'll have to check with Jitka.

SUE: Fine. Can you let me know before Friday?

BERNDT: I'll let you know before then.

Saying 'no' to an invitation

SUE: Michel, I want to try the new vegetarian café across the road. Are you free for lunch on Friday?

MICHEL: I'm afraid I can't. I have some visitors from the US. But thanks for the invitation.

SUE: That's OK. Another time.

MICHEL: Definitely.

Cancelling an invitation

VASILI: I'm really sorry Sue, but I have to cancel lunch tomorrow. Something's come up.

SUE: No problem.

VASILI: Can we fix another time?

SUE: Let's do something next week.

VASILI: Yes, sorry about that.

27.2 T'ai Chi can improve your life

INTERVIEWER: Mike, what is T'ai Chi?

MIKE: T'ai Chi is not Kung Fu or anything like that. The idea of T'ai Chi is very different, it's internal. There are four main elements: firstly, working on the way we breathe; secondly, our body position; thirdly, learning soft movements to help energy and balance; and the final element is meditation, a quiet part, which many people like.

INTERVIEWER: And who comes to your classes?

MIKE: Anybody can come and do it. I have every type of person, from ten years old and I think my oldest student is about 90. All types, all physical types can benefit.

INTERVIEWER: So what are the benefits of T'ai Chi?

MIKE: Well, the main benefit is you just feel good, less stressed. T'ai Chi just helps you to be happier with your life.

INTERVIEWER: And is T'ai Chi better than other things you can do, like sport or being a vegetarian?

MIKE: I'm a vegetarian too but I think T'ai Chi is better than sport because it really makes you think more about your health, and you begin to know what is good and bad for the body. And so for many, T'ai Chi is a beginning and you go on and maybe run a marathon or do some other sporting activities. I think T'ai Chi makes you think – and that's good.

INTERVIEWER: Do you go to companies to do this kind of thing?

MIKE: A little, yes, at some business conferences. And I do stress management courses using T'ai Chi principles. And you can get good results. A simple thing I often say is that you should take two minutes, only two minutes, in the middle of a busy day, just to relax and breathe slowly. Breathing slowly can stop stress and so build energy again for the day.

INTERVIEWER: Can you say in one sentence why I should do T'ai Chi?

MIKE: Why should you do it? Well, it's easy. You should do T'ai Chi because I think it can improve your life!

28 Perfect planning

28.1 Have you organised everything?

JANE: Hi, Anne. How are the plans for the exhibition going?

ANNE: I'm busy, but OK.

JANE: Good. Can I just check a few things? Have you booked the Hilton? I liked it there last time.

ANNE: Yes, I have, and I've asked for rooms with a sea view.

JANE: Great. What about getting to the airport? Have you booked the taxi?

ANNE: Yes, the taxi will pick us up from the office at ten.

JANE: Have you emailed Giulia to cancel the meeting yet?

ANNE: Oh, no. Sorry, not yet. But I've booked La Riviera for Wednesday evening to have dinner with her. I've read that the food is superb and they do fabulous risotto there.

JANE: Great. But could you email her today to confirm?

ANNE: OK, I'll do that immediately. And can I check something? I've organised your meeting with Italia Sports for Thursday. Is that OK?

JANE: Great. Now we can enjoy the trip. Have you ever been to Sicily?

ANNE: No, I haven't but I can't wait. I think it'll be great. Have you?

JANE: Yes, I've been to Sicily twice. The first time was quite romantic …

28.2 Do it yourself

Exercise 2

ANNE: I've got some good news for you. We've received three big new orders. Bob Martin of TXL has ordered our Apollo sports shoe.

JANE: That's excellent. How many has he ordered?

ANNE: Three thousand! Great, isn't it! And ABC and Harcom Sports have also agreed to buy a thousand of our Eagle sports shirts.

JANE: Fantastic. Have you told Peter yet? He'll be delighted.

ANNE: No, I haven't told him yet. I'll phone him later this afternoon.

JANE: And have you spoken to any Japanese buyers?

ANNE: Yes, but no luck! In fact, we've never sold any of our products in Japan. But, despite that, I have to say that the exhibition has been a great success.

JANE: Thanks very much, Anne.

28.3 Sounds good

Exercise 1

Their rooms are very comfortable.
Have you found the receipt?

28.4 Sounds good

Exercise 2

colleague   jewellery   aisle   castle   talked   weight
impatient   dessert   budget   salmon

30 Jets and pets

30.1 Working with animals

INTERVIEWER: So, Gayle, it's good to meet you. Can you tell me what you do?

GAYLE: Well, I have my own business, which is designing, making and selling products for travelling with a pet. OK, so what I do is pet travel.

INTERVIEWER: How did you get this idea?

GAYLE: Well, I changed my lifestyle totally. At the beginning, I was a flight attendant and I travelled all over the world. And then someone gave me a dog called Sherpa but I couldn't take her with me on airplanes. There just wasn't a bag anywhere in the world.

INTERVIEWER: OK, so, that's how you got the idea, and so then you went and started a business?

GAYLE: Well, what I did was some research and then I designed a bag and started to work with a company in Korea on the first, original Sherpa bag.

INTERVIEWER: Tell me a little about the business, how big you are, how many bags you sell, that kind of thing?

GAYLE: Well, I started in 1990 with one thousand bags and now I sell over one hundred thousand a year. And the Sherpa bag is now the standard for travel really in the world I think. So, it's gone from nothing to a four-million dollar company.

INTERVIEWER: That's fantastic. I guess you had to learn a lot in a short time!

GAYLE: It was difficult at first but, you know, we are learning things all through our life and I always try to be a good learner, and to learn interesting things.

INTERVIEWER: So, are you happy you have changed your lifestyle so much? You must be very busy.

GAYLE: Yes, it's very busy. But I'm really happy I've changed. Business is exciting! And if you do something you love, you will have success.

INTERVIEWER: So, with this busy lifestyle, can you still balance life and work?

GAYLE: Sure. You know, I was born and raised on the west coast, in California, and it's a very healthy lifestyle out there. I eat well, a lot of vegetarian food, that kind of thing. But what is really important to me now is yoga. Yoga helps you to relax, it gives you that balance; it is really a part of my life now. Everyone needs to have balance in their lives.

30.2 Saying goodbye

Organising airport transport

A: Linda, when are you leaving?
B: I've ordered a taxi for 1 o'clock.
A: I'm leaving the office early. I can take you to the airport, if you want.
B: That's very kind but I can take a taxi. It's no problem.

Exchanging contact information

A: Here's my business card.
B: Oh, thanks, I'm afraid I don't have one with me.
A: Don't worry.
B: But this is my mobile number and email address.
A: Great. I'll contact you on Monday with the information you want.

Giving a present

A: Before you go, this is for you.
B: What's this?
A: It's a little present to say thank you.
B: It's beautiful. Thank you very much.
A: My pleasure. Thank you.

Saying goodbye

B: I have to go. The taxi's here.
A: Well, it was nice working with you.
B: Yes, the same for me. It was great.
A: Have a good trip back.
B: See you soon, I hope.
A: Take care. Bye.

Revision 2

R2.1 Pronunciation

Exercise 1

1 forty-five
2 a hundred and fifty-four
3 three hundred and thirty-eight
4 four pounds ninety-nine
5 ninety-nine dollars fifty
6 five hundred and sixty-five euros
7 thirty thousand euros
8 sixty-five thousand five hundred dollars
9 two hundred and fifty thousand dollars
10 one million five hundred thousand euros

R2.2 Pronunciation

Exercise 2

A: Are you staying for two or three days?
B: I'm planning to stay for three days.
A: Where are you staying?
B: I'm staying at Vanna's house.
A: Have you been to Italy before?
B: I've been lots of times before!

Answer key

1 Nice to meet you

Warm up
Susie – Masahiko: Less formal
Wollmann – Duroc: More formal

Listen to this
Say who you are

1 Name: Olga Novotna
Visitor from: Russia
Company activity: Sportswear
Action: No action

2 1 T   2 F   3 T   4 F

Check your grammar
The present simple 1
1 do   2 are   3 is   4 am   5 am   6 have   7 do   8 Have

Do it yourself

1 1 Do you work for IBM?
2 Do you have (any) children? / Have you got (any) children?
3 I don't work in Paris.
4 We work near Milan.

2 1 I work for a British company.
2 I come from the north of England originally.
3 I live in Croydon, about 20 kilometres from London.
4 I'm a personal assistant.
5 I go to the US about six times a year on business.

3 1 c   2 e   3 d   4 b   5 a

4 1 are   2 I'm   3 from   4 Do   5 come   6 don't   7 work
8 do   9 make   10 sell

2 Helping people to learn

Read on
A new future

1 1 C   2 D   3 B   4 A

2 1 Helping women to begin in politics and training men and
women
2 Eastern Europe (for example Moldova and Ukraine)
3 Four
4 Meeting people

The words you need ... to talk about your job

1 1 of   2 for   3 in   4 for   5 with   6 of   7 of   8 in

2 1 meet   2 organisation   3 communicate   4 manage
5 discussions

Telephoning 1: Getting information

1 Jake Roberts 1   Cancel training ✗
Call back in ten minutes 1
Jane Dawson 2   Discuss a problem 1
No action – talk next week 2
Julie Simpson ✗   Give help 2
Send email with information ✗

2 A Good morning. How can I help you? (1)
Who's calling, please? (2)
Connecting you now. (1)
I'll put you through. (2)
B It's ... (+ name) (2)
C Could I speak to ... (+ name)? (2)
D I'm just calling to ... (+ reason for call) (2)
Thanks for calling. (1, 2)
Talk to you next week. Bye. (2)

Caller 2 is the better caller. The speaker uses polite greetings
and phrases and has a friendly intonation. All these things
are missing in the first call.

3 Have a good weekend

It's almost the weekend
1 e   2 c   3 b   4 a   5 h   6 g   7 f   8 d

Listen to this
Enjoying your weekend

2 Sally: sailing, walking
Hinawi: sightseeing, swimming
Martina: visiting friends, going to the cinema, clubbing,
walking, swimming
Jochen: astronomy

The words you need ... to talk about your free time

1 Card and board games: draughts
Reading: non-fiction
Music – listening: classical music
Music – playing: the guitar
Culture: ballet
Couch potato: surfing the net
Food: French
Socialising: going on holiday with friends
Housework: ironing

2 expensive / cheap
dangerous / safe
interesting / boring
fast / slow
relaxing / stressful
nice / horrible
healthy / unhealthy
fantastic / terrible
good / bad

4 North and south

Listen to this
A working day in the north … and in the south of Europe

1 Anneli: has lunch at 11; usually finishes work at 5
  Chiara: has lunch at 1; has dinner at 8

2 1 T 2 T 3 F 4 F

Check your grammar
The present simple 2

1 1 does 2 doesn't 3 does 4 is

2

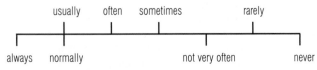

3 1 a/every/per 2 every/each 3 times

Do it yourself

1 1 I normally start work at 7.30.
  2 She travels on business once a year.
  3 How often does she call you?
  4 Do you often speak English at work?

2 1 always 2 every 3 usually 4 times 5 a 6 never

3 2 What time does he finish?
  3 How often does he go to Cuba?
  4 Where does he go at lunchtime?
  5 What does he do at the weekend?

4 1 c 2 b 3 e 4 d 5 a

Sounds good
The present simple third person

Type 1	Type 2	Type 3
/s/	/z/	/ɪz/
writes	leaves	relaxes
works	sells	organises
meets	buys	manages
visits	listens	
	does	

5 Health care – public or private?

Read on
Working at Växjö Hospital

1 1 A 2 C 3 B 4 D

2 1 2,100
  2 To focus on the customer.
  3 250 krona
  4 She likes to look after people and not only think about profit.

The words you need … to talk about people and organisations

1 1 employees 2 competitor 3 customers 4 supplier
  5 consultants

2 1 as 2 after 3 for 4 to 5 at 6 with

Telephoning 2: Taking messages
Can I take a message?

1 1 e 2 b 3 f 4 g

6 Downtown Barcelona

Shopping

1 f 2 h 3 i 4 b 5 e 6 a 7 j 8 g 9 c 10 d

Listen to this
A shoppers' paradise

1 Gaudi: La Pedrera
  Hand-made gifts
  Fine wines
  Fresh food
  Passeig de Gracia

2 1 F 2 F 3 F 4 T

The words you need … to talk about where you live

1 1 in 2 in 3 near 4 outside 5 on 6 from 7 from 8 in

2 1 takes 2 go 3 catch/get 4 walk/get 5 get

7 Changing workspace

Listen to this
This is where I work

1 Fitness centre
  Table games
  Restaurant

2 1 One – the Managing Director
  2 It's flexible so people can work the hours they want to
  3 He gets information more quickly because people talk more
  4 The glass walls – it's not very private and people can see if he is angry

Check your grammar
Countable and uncountable nouns

1 are 2 some 3 any 4 Are 5 Is 6 aren't

Do it yourself

1 1 There are two training rooms on the first floor. / There is a training room on the first floor.
  2 There aren't any private offices on the top floor. / There isn't a private office on the top floor.
  3 Is there any computer equipment on the first floor? / Is there computer equipment on the first floor?
  4 There aren't a lot of spaces in the car park. / There isn't a lot of space in the car park.

2 1 is there 2 there's 3 there's 4 Is there 5 there are
  6 Is there 7 there isn't 8 there are 9 Is there
  10 there are

3 1 some / a lot of 2 some / no 3 any / a lot of 4 any
  5 a lot of / no

Sounds good
Linking

1 3 sounds more natural.

2 1 Telenor is a big company.

  2 It's a very big building.

  3 I think it's very, very flexible.

  4 There's a big fitness centre, which is very good.

  5 Yes, I like it a lot.

8 The A team

Read on
We're a great team

1 1 B 2 E 3 D 4 C 5 A

2 1 John (C) 2 David (D) 3 Katie (E) 4 Jean (B) 5 Jack (A)

The words you need ... to describe people

1 2 creative 3 impatient 4 competitive 5 direct
6 punctual 7 confident

Meeting a visitor at the airport

1 1 arrival 2 flight 3 confirm 4 meet 5 take 6 plan
7 seeing 8 wishes

2 It's good to see you again. How are you?
Did you have a good trip?
Can I help you with your luggage?
The car's in the car park.
How's the weather back home?

9 I love Chicago

Getting around

1 e 2 b 3 g 4 f 5 h 6 d 7 c 8 a

Listen to this
It's my kind of town

1 A Lebanese restaurant
The Sears Tower
Louis Armstrong
The Chicago Cubs
The Taste of Chicago
Al Capone

2 1 T 2 F 3 F 4 T

The words you need ... to talk about city life

1 1 c 2 j 3 h 4 g 5 a 6 i 7 b 8 d 9 f 10 e

2 1 busy / quiet
2 safe / dangerous
3 clean / dirty
4 noisy / quiet
5 high / low
6 warm / cool
7 awful / excellent
8 beautiful / ugly
9 full / empty

10 Eating around the world

Warm up

Morocco: couscous
India: curry
England: roast beef and Yorkshire pudding
Mexico: burritos
France: foie gras

Listen to this
Favourite food

1 England, France and India

2 1 T 2 T 3 F 4 T

Check your grammar
Comparative and superlative adjectives

1 cheaper 2 tastier 3 tastiest 4 most 5 more 6 least
7 best 8 bad

Do it yourself

1 1 I learn vocabulary faster than I learn grammar.
2 For me, English grammar is easier than French grammar.
3 My Spanish is worse than my French.
4 The most important language for international business
is English.

2 1 Fresh fruit is healthier than chocolate.
2 Salmon is cheaper than Russian caviar.
3 Champagne is more expensive than Cava.
4 A sandwich is quicker to eat than a meal in a restaurant.
5 Indian food is spicier than English food.

3 1 The Knightsbridge is **more** expensive than Chez Pierre.
2 Gianni's is the **biggest** restaurant in the guide.
3 The Mogul is **smaller** than Gianni's.
4 Chez Pierre is the **least** expensive / **cheapest** restaurant in
the guide.
5 The Knightsbridge has the **best** food in the guide.

Sounds good
Weak stress 1

2 1 We're _politer_ _than_ _the_ rest.
2 We're fast_er_ _than_ _the_ rest.
3 We're less expensive _than_ _the_ rest.
4 We're _the_ biggest in _the_ world.
5 We're _the_ best in _the_ world.

11 Nice work

Read on
Homeworking

1 1 D 2 B 3 A 4 C

2 1 Gardening; playing football with friends; sitting in the
garden
2 He prefers to work alone; can go directly to his desk with
no traffic problems; liked to look after the children when
they were younger; likes working with his wife
3 His Internet connection
4 He loves working in education and with writing

The words you need ... to talk about work

1 1 from / at 2 at 3 in 4 abroad 5 alone 6 part-time

2 1 d 2 g 3 a 4 f 5 h 6 b 7 c 8 e

Emails 1: Giving your emails a clear structure

1 1 c 2 d 3 b 4 a

2 1 b 2 d 3 c 4 a

3 1 Dear Simon
We are having a meeting with Jayne Keegan in Berlin on
21st January.
Can you meet her at the hotel and drive her over?
Thanks.
(Name)

2 Dear Christine
We need to finalise a price for the XZ34.
Could you call me tomorrow?
Regards
(Name)

3 Dear Karl
There is a production problem in Oslo.
Could you give Henrik a ring on 0047 9843 768767?
Best wishes
(Name)

12 Do you salsa?

I've got news for you

1 g   2 d   3 c   4 h   5 b   6 f   7 a   8 e

Listen to this

I hate watching TV

1   Ben: tennis, squash, motorcycle racing
Alison: flying, scuba diving
Roisin: salsa dancing, swimming

2   Ben: Winning is not important. I like to socialise.
Alison: It's good exercise. I like being alone.
Roisin: I have to relax after work. I hate sport on TV.

The words you need ... to talk about sport

1   1 lost   2 played / beat   3 won   4 beat   5 won

2   play   ice hockey, golf, football
do   (some / a lot of) running, yoga, aerobics, gymnastics, cycling, swimming, walking, weight training, skiing
go   running, cycling, swimming, walking, skiing

3   Football
0 – 0   nil – nil
1 – 0   one – nil
1 – 1   one – all (one – one)
2 – 1   two – one
Tennis
15 – 0   fifteen – love
15 – 15   fifteen – all
30 – 15   thirty – fifteen
40 – 40   deuce

4   A tennis match is decided by the winner of the bigger number of sets. Women usually play three sets and men play three or five sets. A set is won by reaching six games by two clear games or by winning 7 – 6 in a tie-break. In some matches, the last set is not decided by a tie-break and will continue until one player establishes a two-game lead. Note that 'game' can also sometimes mean 'match'.

13 Chanel

Listen to this

Gabrielle (Coco) Chanel – inventor of the fashion industry

1   a 1946   b 1971   c 1910   d 1924   e 1921   f 1883   g 1954

2   1 From the name of a song which she sang.
2 It was the fifth perfume they tested.
3 He held a fashion show for her.
4 She created the two-piece suit for women.

Check your grammar

The past simple

1 was   2 weren't   3 wasn't   4 Were   5 did   6 arrived
7 didn't   8 got   9 went   10 had

Do it yourself

1   1 I did it yesterday.
2 I didn't have time.
3 Were you busy?
4 What did you do last night?

2   1 was   2 started   3 left   4 didn't want   5 graduated
6 joined   7 stayed   8 left   9 launched   10 were

3   1 was   2 grow   3 did   4 study   5 join   6 long   7 stay

4   1 do   2 went   3 did   4 was   5 wasn't   6 didn't

Sounds good

The past simple

2

/t/	/d/	/ɪd/
liked	enjoyed	decided
decreased	received	wanted
looked	listened	visited
increased		
talked		
walked		

14 Médecins Sans Frontières

Read on

Médecins Sans Frontières – working to help people

1   1 D   2 A   3 C   4 B

2   1 Over 30 years ago
2 Gives medical help to people in wars and natural disasters. It also tells the world about them.
3 The three centres are in Brussels, Paris and Barcelona but they also work in 85 other countries.
4 She communicates important information about medicine to people in India and Africa.

The words you need ... to talk about your organisation

1   1 started   2 headquarters   3 based   4 offices   5 active
6 department

2   1 gives   2 publishes   3 supplies   4 makes   5 sells
6 provides

Visiting an organisation

Step 1
1 appointment   2 tell   3 sign   4 course   5 moment
6 could   7 badge
Step 2
Nice to meet you.
Please follow me.
Is this your first trip to London?
Here we are.
Please take a seat.
Can I get you a drink?
250 people work in this building.

15 Trekking in Nepal

Getting there

1 c   2 e   3 j   4 f   5 d   6 h   7 b   8 i   9 a   10 g

Listen to this

Walking at 5,000 metres

1   When: 10 years ago
Number of days walking: 25 days
Distance walked every day: 18 kilometres
Size of trekking group: 2

2   1 The air was very thin so sometimes there wasn't enough oxygen
2 Rucksack, sleeping bag and warm clothing
3 Rice, potatoes, vegetables
4 The walking, the exercise, the countryside, the clean air and the quiet

The words you need ... for holidays and travel

1   1 Do   2 Go   3 Sit   4 Hire   5 Relax   6 Take

2   1 by   2 took   3 late   4 rank   5 trolley   6 attendant
7 missed   8 flight

Revision 1: Units 1–15

Grammar
1 1 What do you do?
   2 Which company do you work for?
   3 Where does she come from?
   4 Do you do much sport at the weekend?
   5 What did you do last night?
   6 What did you have to eat?
   7 Did you have a good trip?
   8 How long did it take to get here?
2 1 Are there a lot of restaurants near your office? / Is there a restaurant near your office?
   2 Is there a lot of information on your website?
   3 Are there a lot of people who need English for their job?
   4 I think English grammar is easier than Russian grammar.
   5 Gucci clothes are generally more expensive than clothes from Marks & Spencer.
   6 I think the weather today is worse than yesterday.

General vocabulary
1 quiet – noisy
   clean – dirty
   empty – full
   safe – dangerous
   beautiful – ugly
   low – high
2 1 relax   2 do   3 go   4 play   5 get   6 drive

Business communication
1 1 speak   2 Who's   3 put   4 can   5 calling   6 See
2 1 Dear   2 send   3 Attached   4 information
   5 contact/call   6 Best

Pronunciation
1 1 We have a message for you.
   2 It's about our company.
   3 It's a great place to work.
   4 We need another 50 people.
   5 So, come and join us.
2 /t/   /d/   /ɪd/
   liked   played   needed
   decreased   enjoyed   decided
   looked   listened   visited
   walked

Business vocabulary
1 1 offices   2 industry   3 started   4 headquarters
   5 based   6 responsible
2 1 customer   2 employer   3 competitor   4 employee
   5 supplier   6 consultant

Social phrases
1 1 d   2 e   3 a   4 c   5 b   6 f
2 *Possible answers*
   1 How are you?
   2 Could I have a receipt, please? / Could you give me a receipt, please?
   3 Would you like some/a coffee?
   4 Keep the change.
   5 How much is this/that?
   6 Have a good weekend.

16 Project Stockholm

Listen to this
What project are you working on at the moment?
1 Number of workers: 200
   Location: Stockholm city centre
   Architect: Norman Foster
   Project: Building a new bridge
2 1 T   2 F   3 T   4 F

Check your grammar
The present continuous 1

1 are   2 working   3 not   4 is   5 staying   6 is   7 aren't
8 not   9 am   10 not

Do it yourself
1 Jane: Where are you staying this week? In a hotel?
   Riggert: Yes, I'm staying in a little hotel near the conference centre.
   Jane: So, are you enjoying the conference?
   Riggert: No, I'm not enjoying it. I hate conferences!
2 1 designs; are designing   2 produces
   3 are launching   4 am running   5 work; are working
3 1 are you working on
   2 are/'re reorganising
   3 isn't working
   4 am/'m working
   5 don't like
   6 are/'re developing
   7 are travelling
   8 go

Sounds good
Sentence stress

1 All three sentences can take about the same time to say.
2 A: Are you <u>working</u> from <u>home</u> <u>next</u> <u>week</u>?
   B: Yes, I'm <u>working</u> from <u>home</u> to the <u>end</u> of the <u>month</u>.
   A: Are you <u>busy</u>?
   B: <u>Yes</u>, but I'm <u>enjoying</u> the <u>work</u>.
3 2 Are you reading a good book at the moment?
   3 Are you enjoying the lesson?
   4 What are you doing?
   5 Are you having a good time?

17 Workplace communication

Read on
Communication of the future

1 1 C   2 A   3 D   4 B
2 1 For marketing meetings
   2 There is a delay with the voice, so you wait after people speak to hear the words.
   3 Because it's face-to-face and therefore more personal
   4 You have to buy a lot of equipment.

The words you need ... to talk about communication
1 1 talk   2 explain   3 ask   4 interrupt   5 listening
   6 contact   7 call
2 1 discuss   2 speaks   3 listens to   4 replies to   5 reads
   6 calls   7 asks   8 interrupts

Emails 2: Replying to emails

1 1 Greeting: Hi Jan
   2 Polite beginning: Thanks for your email and the attached report.
   3 Information/Action point: I'll read it over the weekend and call you on Monday.
   4 Close: Enjoy the weekend.

2 1 d 2 a 3 b 4 c

3 *Possible answers*
Dear Sam
Here is another copy of the report I sent last week.
Best wishes
Frank

Dear Adrian
Klara has told me that you have kindly passed on a possible new customer for me, John Peters. I am very grateful and will contact John soon.
Kind regards
Frank

18 Slow food
Restaurant talk

1 1 i 2 b 3 d 4 f 5 e 6 h 7 j 8 a 9 g 10 c

Listen to this
A great place to eat

1 1 was established in Italy in 1986
   2 became international in 1989
   3 is against intensive farming
   4 prefers food which is local and simple
   5 wants to see good service in restaurants

2 1 The movement was started after the opening of a McDonald's restaurant in Rome, Italy.
   2 Wendy thinks that intensive farming is bad for animals, bad for the taste of meat, and maybe bad for our health.
   3 From local producers
   4 Slow means good – good **food** and good **service**.

The words you need … for eating and drinking

1 1 dish 2 plate 3 starter 4 dessert 5 cuisine
2 1 meat 2 seafood 3 fish 4 vegetables 5 fruit
   6 drinks

19 Living in Hong Kong
Listen to this
Chinese culture

1 1 F 2 T 3 T 4 F

2 1 An older and more traditional Hong Kong and a younger, more westernised Hong Kong
   2 Because modern houses and flats are so small
   3 Ten or 15 per cent, or more if you're very happy with the service
   4 Because people sometimes get into the train before other people have the chance to get out

Check your grammar
Should and *have to*

1 b 2 d 3 c 4 a

Do it yourself

1 1 You don't have to use surnames with the younger generation in Hong Kong.

---

   2 You shouldn't disagree with your boss in a meeting.
   3 Should I dress formally for the meeting? / Do I have to dress formally for the meeting?
   4 He shouldn't smoke in here. People are trying to eat.

2 1 have to 2 don't have to 3 should 4 has to
   5 shouldn't

3 1 b 2 f 3 d 4 a 5 c 6 e

Sounds good
Word stress

2 1 fan<u>tas</u>tic 2 dy<u>nam</u>ic 3 tra<u>di</u>tional 4 <u>mon</u>ey
   5 <u>fash</u>ionable 6 im<u>por</u>tant 7 <u>mod</u>ern 8 per <u>cent</u>

20 Online
Read on
Computer heaven or hell?

1 1 D 2 B 3 A 4 C

2 1 Over 50.
   2 They hate shopping in real shops and it's easy to use.
   3 Schoolwork, chatting to friends and learning Spanish.
   4 Over 12 hours.

The words you need … to talk about computers and the Internet

1 1 log on 2 created 3 saved 4 print 5 resend
   1 c 2 a 3 b

2 1 connect 2 online 3 intranet 4 surf 5 virus 6 chat

Telephoning 3: Arranging meetings

1 Philippe – Friday – 14.00
Frank – Monday – 13.00
Petra – Tuesday – 10.00

2 Is it possible to have a meeting?
When are you free?
See you next week.
I'm calling to fix a meeting.
I'm sorry, I can't.
See you on Tuesday at 10.

21 Beirut Intercontinental
Enjoy your stay

1 1 g 2 h 3 e 4 f 5 b 6 i 7 j 8 d 9 c 10 a

Listen to this
It's a great place to stay

1 Hotel 3
2 1 F 2 F 3 T 4 F

The words you need … for staying in hotels

1 1 key 2 cancel 3 recommend 4 double room
   5 towels 6 change 7 corridor 8 connect
2 1 b 2 a 3 e 4 d 5 c

22 Working for Rolls Royce
Listen to this
Work is like a second home

1 Number of employees: 4
Meetings per week: 2–3
Working hours per week: 35
Holiday weeks per year: 6

2 1 She makes herself a big cup of coffee.
2 75–80% of her time
3 She has six weeks' holiday, but no other benefits.
4 She likes working for a British company; she speaks English a lot; she feels part of a team.

Check your grammar
Many, much, a few, a little

1 a few   **2** much   **3** many   **4** a little

Do it yourself

1 1 I don't give many presentations in my job.
2 Do you want a little milk with your coffee?
3 How much information do you have about our new product?
4 I'm sorry but I need a little more time to write this report.

2 1 many   **2** much   **3** many   **4** much   **5** many   **6** many
7 much   **8** many

3 1 a lot of / a few   **2** much / a lot of   **3** a little
4 a few   **5** many

Sounds good
Saying numbers and prices

Numbers

25	twenty-five
100	a hundred *or* one hundred
101	a hundred and one *or* one hundred and one
1,000	a thousand *or* one thousand
2,001	two thousand and one
10,550	ten thousand five hundred and fifty
500,000	five hundred thousand
1,000,000	a million *or* one million
1,000,000,000	a billion *or* one billion

Prices

50p	fifty p
£4.99	four pounds ninety-nine p *or* four pounds ninety-nine
£250	two hundred and fifty pounds
€150,000	a hundred and fifty thousand euros *or* one hundred and fifty thousand euros
£150m	a hundred and fifty million pounds *or* one hundred and fifty million pounds
$0.99	ninety-nine cents
$4.95	four dollars ninety-five cents *or* four dollars ninety-five
$2,500	two thousand five hundred dollars
$2.5m	two point five million dollars *or* two and a half million dollars

23 Start up

Read on
Managing a small business

1 1 D   **2** E   **3** B   **4** A   **5** C

2 1 Four years ago
2 A member of their family lent them the money.
3 Fresh fruit and vegetables
4 Profits doubled (they increased by 100%).
5 Because they can make more money this way: the margins are higher

The words you need ... to talk about money and business finance

1 1 turnover   **2** profit   **3** costs   **4** margin   **5** budget
2 1 make   **2** borrow   **3** increase   **4** invest   **5** pay

Helping visitors

1 1 b   **2** c   **3** d   **4** a

2 Follow me.
Do you want to borrow some money?
Would you like to use a computer here?
I can show you on the map if you want.

24 I buy money
Money talk

1 1 i   **2** d   **3** e   **4** g   **5** c   **6** j   **7** a   **8** h   **9** f   **10** b

Listen to this
Hey, big spender

1 1 b   **2** c   **3** a

2 1 **On** Saturday mornings
2 For holidays
3 Old coins
4 No. He spends without thinking.
5 Belgian chocolate
6 Almost every month

The words you need ... to talk about money

1 1 on   **2** in   **3** for   **4** by   **5** for   **6** with
2 1 generous   **2** notes   **3** get   **4** reasonable

25 Driving to Romania
Listen to this
A job everyone wants to do

1 1 F   **2** F   **3** T   **4** F

2 1 He saw a lot of television programmes about Romanian children's homes and wanted to help.
2 To make the children's homes a better place to live
3 To build a hospital
4 Nothing – they are volunteers

Check your grammar
The present continuous 2

1 doing   **2** are / 're   **3** Are   **4** am   **5** aren't / 're not

Do it yourself

1 1 I'm giving a presentation next week.
2 Is your boss coming to the meeting?
3 Are you going to the theatre tonight?
4 I'm not coming to the theatre tonight. I'm tired.

2 1 we're not meeting / we aren't meeting
2 We're seeing
3 when are you going
4 we're running
5 Are you still coming
6 we're having

3 *Model answer*

From:

To: Kim Copeland

Subject: Workshop

Dear Kim

Thank you for your email. Regarding the workshop:

1 Participants

Anna Parkland and Harald Henrikssen are coming.
Johan Meier isn't coming because he's too busy.

2 Speakers

Jessica Langer is talking about Quality Management on Tuesday at 10.00.
Thomas Salter is talking about Selling on Wednesday at 09.00.
I don't have any confirmation from the other speakers.

3 Evening programme

On Tuesday evening, we're going to the opera.
On Wednesday evening, we're seeing a Shakespeare play at Stratford.

Please contact me if you have any more questions.

Best regards

Sounds good

Weak stress 2

1 Example 2 sounds more natural.

2 and 3

A: What <u>are</u> you doing next week?
B: I'm going <u>to</u> Poland.
A: Pol<u>and</u>? What <u>are</u> you doing there?
B: I'm visiting <u>a</u> friend.
A: How long <u>are</u> you staying?
B: Just <u>for a</u> few days.
A: When <u>are</u> you coming back?
B: Next Friday.
A: <u>Are</u> you doing anything <u>at the</u> weekend?
B: Yes, I'm going camping.

It's time to talk

The only time when three members of the management team can meet is on Wednesday morning.

26 Out of order

Read on

Problems in Pennsylvania

1 1 D   2 B   3 C   4 A

2 1 She telephoned a travel agent friend.
2 It was overcooked and cold.
3 She forgot to switch it on.
4 A 25% discount

The words you need ... to talk about work problems

1 solve; tell (someone about); explain; deal with

2 1 technical   2 time   3 time   4 technical   5 technical   6 time

3 1 You should / need to   2 You should / need to   3 Try   4 You need   5 Try   6 You need

Telephoning 4: Solving problems by phone

1 I'm having a problem
2 Could you get someone
3 I'll ask
4 Is that OK?

5 I didn't get
6 Could you send
7 I'll do
8 Call me back in 30 minutes if you still haven't got it.
9 I can't remember
10 Could you contact
11 I'll call
12 Do you want me to call back after I speak to him?

27 Teaching T'ai Chi

Inviting

1 1 e   2 d   3 b   4 c   5 j   6 f   7 g   8 h   9 a   10 i

Listen to this

T'ai Chi can improve your life

1 1 T   2 F   3 T   4 F

2 1 Meditation
2 You feel good / less stressed.
3 It makes you think about your health and your body.
4 Relax and breathe slowly.

The words you need ... to talk about health

1 1 e   2 c   3 a   4 b   5 f   6 d

2 1 lose   2 stop   3 do   4 reduce   5 relax   6 go

28 Perfect planning

Listen to this

Have you organised everything?

1 The taxi is for 10 am
The Italia Sports meeting is on Thursday
Dinner with Giulia is on Wednesday evening

2 1 T   2 F   3 T   4 F

Check your grammar

The present perfect

1 booked   **2** haven't   **3** Has   **4** been   **5** have   **6** hasn't

Do it yourself

1 1 I've done it. / I did it last week.
2 She hasn't finished the report.
3 Have you (ever) been to Italy?
4 I haven't received any emails so far today.

2 2 has ordered
3 has he ordered
4 have also agreed
5 Have you told
6 haven't told
7 have you spoken to
8 've never sold / have never sold
9 has been

29 A changing world

Read on

A year in Germany

1 1 D   2 C   3 A   4 B

2 1 Unemployment in eastern Germany increased.
2 The price of some of Frank's products decreased a little last year.
3 Bayer's market share increased a little.
4 Frank's work has increased a lot.

The words you need ... to talk about change

1 1 d   2 c   3 a   4 e   5 b

2 1 decreased   2 has risen   3 fell   4 have increased
   5 went up

Emails 3: Arranging meetings by email

1 1 c   2 d   3 a   4 b

2 1 meet   2 by   3 forward   4 can't   5 make

30 Jets and pets

Listen to this

Working with animals

1 1 T   2 T   3 F   4 T

2 1 She couldn't find a travelling bag for her dog, Sherpa.
   2 Four million dollars
   3 A good learner
   4 She does yoga.

The techniques you need ... for learning vocabulary

1 Work: C   Internet: A   Health: B

2 1 a meeting   2 money   3 emails   4 a car

3 1 organised   2 organisation   3 organise

Saying goodbye

1 1 c   2 d   3 h   4 j   5 g   6 f   7 i   8 e   9 a   10 b

Revision 2: Units 16–30

Grammar

1 1 What do you do?
   2 Where are you staying?
   3 What are you doing tonight?
   4 Have you been to Edinburgh before?
   5 When did you go? / When was that? / When were you last here?

2 1 have increased   2 has risen   3 fell   4 have stayed
   5 has gone up   6 went down

3 1 much   2 a few   3 many

4 1 should   2 have to / should   3 don't have to

General vocabulary

1 1 meat   2 a dessert   3 dish   4 wine list   5 main course
   6 bill

2 1 spend   2 save   3 borrow   4 lend   5 pay   6 get

Business communication

1 1 thanks   2 apologise   3 agenda   4 forward   5 wishes

2 1 fix   2 discuss   3 convenient   4 what   5 confirm   6 see

Pronunciation

1 1 45   6 €565
   2 154   7 €30,000
   3 338   8 $65,500
   4 £4.99   9 $250,000
   5 $99.50   10 €1,500,000

2 A: Are you <u>staying</u> for <u>two</u> or <u>three</u> days?
   B: I'm <u>planning</u> to <u>stay</u> for <u>three</u> days.
   A: <u>Where</u> are you <u>staying</u>?
   B: I'm <u>staying</u> at <u>Vanna's</u> <u>house</u>.
   A: Have you <u>been</u> to <u>Italy</u> <u>before</u>?
   B: I've been <u>lots</u> of <u>times</u> <u>before</u>!

Business vocabulary

1 turnover   2 costs   3 finance   4 budget   5 profit   6 margin

Social phrases

1 1 d   2 e   3 b   4 f   5 a   6 c

2   2 B: Before you go, Annette. This is a little present just to say thank you.
   3 A: Oh, my favourite chocolates. Thank you very much.
   4 B: My pleasure.
   5 A: I shall eat these on the plane. OK, Ian, thank you again for everything.
   6 B: No problem. It was good to have you here.
   7 A: Take care. See you next month.
   8 B: Yes. Have a good trip. Bye.

Thanks and acknowledgements

The authors would like to thank:
- Bonnie Bernström, Sally Searby, Jihad Hinawi, Martina Hruba, Jochen Lohmeyer, Anneli Ejnestrand, Chiara Nesler, Margita Westring, Montse Benet, Stein Idar Stokke, Ellen Zlotnick, Ablaziz Esseid, Paul Munden (National Association of Writers in Education, UK), Ben Ashcroft, Alison Collings, Roisin Vaughan, Polly Markandya and the kind permission of Petrana Nowill, Pres Officer of Médecins Sans Frontières (www.msf.org), Jürgen Robbert, Riggert Andersson, Paula Morris, Wendy Fogarty (www.slowfood.com), John Duncan, Bob Hands, Isabelle Segura, Jackie and Phil Black (Tower Street Pantry, York, UK), Tashi Ugyen, Anthony Allen (www.sroauk.org.uk), Mike Tabrett, Frank Hatke, Gayle Martz, Sarah Schechter and the students of Anglia Polytechnic University, and the students and teachers of Eurocentre, Cambridge for their help with interviews;
- the interviewees for their photographs;
- Ian Chitty, Graham Ditchfield, Eryl Griffiths, Robert Highton, Bernie Hayden, Jackie Mann, Francis O'Hara, Duncan Nicholson, Chaz Pugliese and Elizabetta Trebar for reviewing the material in its early stages;
- Will Capel and Sally Searby of Cambridge University Press for their unflinching support from start to finish;
- Alison Silver for her eagle eye for detail, for her good sense and good cheer throughout the editorial and proofreading process;
- Hilary Fletcher for the picture research and Ruth Carim for proofreading;
- James Richardson for producing the recordings at Studio AVP, London;
- Hart McLeod for the design and page make-up;
- Sue Evans; Lorenza, Mathieu, Jérôme and Michael Flinders; and Lyn, Jude, Ruth and Neil Sweeney for their patience;
- colleagues and friends at York Associates and in the School of Management, Community and Communication at York St John College for their tolerance of authorial distraction;
- and Chris Capper of Cambridge University Press for his immeasurable contribution to the project. It is above all his huge efforts which have made this book possible.

The authors and publisher are grateful to the following for permission to use copyright material. While every effort has been made, it has not been possible to identify the sources of all the material used and in such cases the publisher would welcome information from the copyright owners:

The publishers are grateful to the following for permission to reproduce copyright photographs and material:

Key: l = left, c = centre, r = right, t = top, b = bottom, back = background).

©ACE for pp. 24 (t), 52; Advertising Archive for p. 45 (tr); Alamy/BananaStock for p. 13, /Tony Perrottet for p. 14 (bl), /Jon Mitchell for p. 25 (fish), /plainpicture/Kirch.S for p. 27 (bl), /popperfoto p. 34, /Burke/Triolo/Brand X Pictures p. 34,/ (Capone), /Robert Harding World Imagery for p. 72 (tl), /Jackson Smith for p 81, /BananaStock for p. 81/Ian Mckinnell for p. 89 (back), /Image Source for p100, /John Foxx for p.100; AP Photos ©Michael S Green for p. 34; CEPHAS/Mick Rock for p. 25 (wine); /©Christian Aid www.christian-aid.org.uk for p. 48; Corbis /©Duomo for p. 9, /©Dave G. Houser for p. 23/ ©Despotovic Dusko/Corbis Sygma for p. 25, /©Laura Doss for p. 42, /©Chuck Savage for p.71, /©Bernard Bisson/Corbis Sygma for p. 81 EMPICS/©Tony Marshall for p. 44 (t); Gareth Bowden for pp. 10, 11, 24, 59, 62, 78, 80 and 89; Greg Evans International Photo Library/Greg Balfour Evans for pp. 14 (bc), 27 (br), 29 (b), 35; ©Ericsson www.ericsson.com for p. 49; Getty Images/ ©Chris M. Rogers/Imagebank for p.9, / GettyImages/Hulton Archive for pp. 14 (back), 47, /Keystone for p. 22, /Macmahon for p 100 (back); GettyImages/Imagebank/ Grant V.Faint for p. 18 (r), /Deborah Jaffe for pp. 30, 31 (tl), /Adrian Weinbrecht for p. 31 (cr), /AJA Productions for p. 31 (bl), /Steven Biver for p. 31 (br), /Bob Stefko for p. 33 (back), /Macduff Everton for p. 36, /Jerry Driendl for p. 38 (c), /Alexander Stewart for p. 51 (back), /Romilly Lockyer for pp. 51 (bcl), 71 (br), /Tom Hussey for p. 51 (bcr), /Stephen Mallon for p. 51 (br), /Wendy Chan for p. 66, /Bruce Ayres/Stone for p. 68, /John & Lisa Merrill for p. 71 (back), /Foto World for p. 85, /Stephen Derr for p. 92; GettyImages/News and Sport/Jamie McDonald for p. 25 (Nou Camp); GettyImages/PhotoDisc/Photo Link for p. 15 (back), /Doug Menuez for p. 27, /Hisham F. Ibrahim for p. 33 (br); GettyImages/Photographers Choice/Naile Goelbasi for p. 31 (cl); GettyImages/Stone/Catherine Ledner for p. 14 (br), /Klaus Lahnstein for p. 25 (La Pedrera), /Amwell for p. 27 (bc), /Peter Pearson for p. 34 (Sears Tower), /Vince Streano for p. 38 (r), /Keith Brofsky for p. 50, /Thomas Del Brase for p. 62 (back), /Charles Gupton for p. 67, /Stewart Cohen for p. 71 (bcl), Paul Chesley for p. 80 (back), /Steven Peters for p. 94; GettyImages/Taxi/V.C.L for pp. 17, 51 (bl), /CHABRUKEN for p. 19, /David Lees for p. 31 (tr), /KAZ CHIBA for p. 32, /Chris Ladd for p. 38 (l), /Travel Pix for p. 65 (b), /David Noton for p. 65 (c), /Robert Brimson for p. 71 (bl), /REZA ESTAKHRIAN for p. 86, /EDUARDO GARCIA for p. 95b, /Stephen Simpson for p. 97; Ronald Grant Archive for pp. 60 (b), 93; ©HONDA www.honda.co.uk for p. 49; ©David Innes for p. 82; ©Le Vendome International, Beruit for p. 72 (br); ©Médecins Sans Frontières www.msf.org for p. 48; ©NEWSCAST for p 20; ©NOKIA www.nokia.com for p. 49; ©OXFAM www.oxfam.org.uk for p. 48; PA Photos/DPA for p. 45 (tl), /ABACA for p. 45 (bl); ©Popperfoto.com for pp. 34 (Armstrong, Ali), 44 (b), 45 (bc); ©Powerstock for pp. 9(b), 18 (l), 25 (Passeig de Gracia) and 100; Reeve photography for p. 23; Rex Features for pp. 45 (br), 46; ©St John www.stjohnrestaurant.com for p. 63; ©TESCO for p. 49; ©Travel Ink/Phil Robinson for p. 25 (olympic), /Andrew Brown for p. 33 (bl, tr), /Pauline Thorton for p. 34 (bus), /Abbie Enock for p. 72 (bl); View/©Grant Smith for p. 29 (t); ©World Wildlife Fund www.wwf.org.uk for p. 48. p.45 The listening text is based on the article on Chanel by Rebecca Hoar, published in *Eurobusiness Magazine* May 2000 © European Press Ltd;

Illustrations:
Loise Wallace; pages 16, 42, 43, 81
Richard Deverall; pages 16, 26, 30, 37, 40, 53, 57, 58, 69, 73, 85, 88, 95
Tim Oliver; pages 32, 34, 37, 44, 64, 96
Linda Combi; pages 10, 28, 39, 40, 66, 68, 75, 79, 86, 88, 90